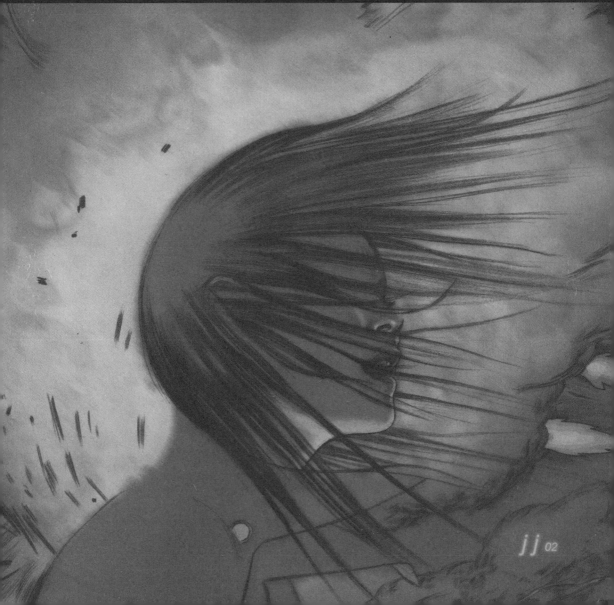

FABLES: ANIMAL FARM

Bill Willingham writer **Mark Buckingham** penciller **Steve Leialoha** inker

Daniel Vozzo colorist **Todd Klein** letterer **James Jean** original series covers

FABLES CREATED BY BILL WILLINGHAM

jj 02

SHELLY BOND Executive Editor – Vertigo and Editor – Original Series **MARIAH HUEHNER** Assistant Editor – Original Series **SCOTT NYBAKKEN** Editor
ROBBIN BROSTERMAN Design Director – Books **HANK KANALZ** Senior VP – Vertigo & Integrated Publishing **DIANE NELSON** President
DAN DIDIO AND JIM LEE Co-Publishers **GEOFF JOHNS** Chief Creative Officer **AMIT DESAI** Senior VP – Marketing & Franchise Management
AMY GENKINS Senior VP – Business & Legal Affairs **NAIRI GARDINER** Senior VP – Finance **JEFF BOISON** VP – Publishing Planning
MARK CHIARELLO VP – Art Direction & Design **JOHN CUNNINGHAM** VP – Marketing **TERRI CUNNINGHAM** VP – Editorial Administration
LARRY GANEM VP – Talent Relations & Services **ALISON GILL** Senior VP – Manufacturing & Operations
JAY KOGAN VP – Business & Legal Affairs, Publishing **JACK MAHAN** VP – Business Affairs, Talent **NICK NAPOLITANO** VP – Manufacturing Administration
SUE POHJA VP – Book Sales **FRED RUIZ** VP – Manufacturing Operations **COURTNEY SIMMONS** Senior VP – Publicity **BOB WAYNE** Senior VP – Sales

FABLES: ANIMAL FARM

Published by DC Comics. Cover, compilation, and character sketches Copyright © 2003 DC Comics. All Rights Reserved.
Originally published in single magazine form as FABLES 6-10. Copyright © 2002, 2003 Bill Willingham and DC Comics. All Rights Reserved.
All characters, their distinctive likenesses and related elements featured in this publication are trademarks of Bill Willingham.
VERTIGO is a trademark of DC Comics. The stories, characters and incidents featured in this publication are entirely fictional.
DC Comics does not read or accept unsolicited submissions of ideas, stories or artwork.

DC Comics, 4000 Warner Blvd., Burbank, CA 91522
A Warner Bros. Entertainment Company.
Printed in Canada. Twelfth Printing.
ISBN: 978-1-4012-0077-0
Cover illustration by James Jean.

This one is dedicated to two of my favorite talking animals, Matt and Mark, past partners in the Tick Tock enterprise,
and friends faithful and true.

— Bill Willingham

Library of Congress Cataloging-in-Publication Data

Willingham, Bill.
  Fables. Vol. 2, Animal farm / Bill Willingham, Mark Buckingham, Steve Leialoha.
    p. cm.
  "Originally published in single magazine form as Fables 6-10."
  ISBN 978-1-4012-0077-0
  1. Legends--Adaptations--Comic books, strips, etc. 2. Graphic novels. I. Buckingham, Mark. II. Leialoha, Steve. III. Title. IV. Title: Animal farm.
  PN6727.W52F383 2012
  741.5'973–dc23
                            2012039379

The Story So Far:

We learned that many characters from the lands of fable and folklore have been hiding out in New York City in an underground community they call *Fabletown*. They're a secret society of refugees from terrible wars, because someone known only as "The Adversary" had methodically invaded and conquered all of their myriad kingdoms, one by one. The Fables--as they call themselves--who cannot pass as human in the city are forced to stay hidden away in the upstate Fabletown annex known as *The Farm*.

Recently, Rose Red and her no-good boyfriend, Jack of the Tales, got caught attempting to fake Rose's murder as part of a scheme to swindle Lord Bluebeard out of a small fortune. Bigby Wolf, the sheriff of Fabletown, earned quite a feather in his cap for solving that one. Snow White, the assistant mayor (and real power behind the throne) sentenced her wayward sister Rose and Jack to many hours of community service, to pay for their crimes. Along the way, Jack was briefly a prince, Prince Charming was briefly a pauper, and many other interesting things occurred.

YES, IT'S "ONCE UPON A TIME" TIME AGAIN.

LISTEN *UP*, JACK.

BIGBY IS IN *TOTAL* CHARGE OF YOU WHILE ROSE AND I ARE GONE THIS WEEK. *DON'T* GIVE HIM ANY *TROUBLE*.

OH, JACK WON'T GIVE *ME* ANY TROUBLE, SNOW, OR I'LL JUST KEEP ADDING TO HIS COMMUNITY SERVICE HOURS.

YOU CAN'T *DO* THAT, BIGBY!

TRY ME, MULCHHEAD.

HE *CAN* AND HE *WILL*, WITH MY *BLESSING*. UNTIL YOU WORK OFF THE LAST OF YOUR PUNISHMENT, JACK, YOU BELONG TO *US*, BODY *AND* SOUL.

DON'T *EVEN* TRY TESTING IT, OR DARK JUDGMENT WILL COME DOWN ON YOU LIKE THE WRATH OF GOD ALMIGHTY.

ROAD TRIP
Part One of Animal Farm

Written by **Bill Willingham** Pencilled by **Mark Buckingham** Inked by **Steve Leialoha**

Lettered by **Todd Klein** Colored and Separated by **Daniel Vozzo**

Cover art by **James Jean** Assistant Editor **Mariah Huehner** Editor **Shelly Bond**

FABLES is created by **Bill Willingham**

WE'LL BE **FINE.** YOU AND ROSE ENJOY YOUR TRIP AND PUT US **ENTIRELY** OUT OF YOUR MIND.

THAT'S **ANOTHER** THING. ROSE AND I GOT THE **SAME** PUNISHMENT.

WHY DOES **SHE** GET TO WORK OFF HER HOURS GOING ON A NICE **VACATION,** WHILE I HAVE TO PULL **JANITORIAL** DUTY ALONGSIDE THIS **INBRED GEEK?**

HEY! DON'T BE SO **MEAN!**

ROSE WON'T BE GOING **ANYWHERE** IF SHE DOESN'T HURRY UP.

NOTHING **PERSONAL,** FLYCATCHER.

PING!

THERE YOU ARE.

YOU'D BE INBRED **TOO** IF YOU HAD TO MARRY INSIDE YOUR OWN **FAMILY** FOR TWENTY GENERATIONS. COUNT YOURSELF **LUCKY** YOU DIDN'T HOLD ONTO YOUR PRINCELY TITLE MORE THAN A DAY.

WHY AREN'T YOU **PACKED** YET? WE'RE **ALREADY** RUNNING LATE.

I **AM** PACKED, SISTER DEAR. THIS IS **IT.**

FOR AN ENTIRE **WEEK**?

I TRAVEL LIGHT.

HAVE FUN. BE CAREFUL. DON'T **KILL** EACH OTHER.

HEY! ROSE BUSH, AREN'T YOU GOING TO...?

SHE DIDN'T EVEN SAY **GOODBYE**. SHE ACTED LIKE I WASN'T EVEN **HERE**

THAT'S BECAUSE, FOR ALL OF HER JERKY WAYS, ROSE IS **STILL** A BRIGHT GIRL--SMART ENOUGH TO FINALLY **REALIZE** YOU HAVE THE STINK OF "LOSER" ALL OVER YOU, JACK.

NOW GET BACK TO WORK. AND WHEN YOU'RE **DONE** WITH THIS, STRIP AND WAX THE BALLROOM FLOOR UPSTAIRS. FLYCATCHER IS IN CHARGE.

WHY DOES **HE** GET TO BE BOSS?

BECAUSE **I** SAID SO.

AND I HAVE THE **EXPERIENCE** TO BE BOSS. I DO THIS WORK ALL THE TIME. I **KNOW** WHAT NEEDS TO BE DONE.

WHAT'S **YOUR** STORY ANYWAY, FLY? WHY ARE YOU ALWAYS STUCK ON COMMUNITY SERVICE?

BIGBY KEEPS CATCHING ME EATING FLIES IN **PUBLIC**. IT'S NOT MANY HOURS' PUNISHMENT FOR EACH OFFENSE, BUT IT ADDS **UP**.

SO WHY **IS** IT THAT I GET TO GO ON THIS TRIP WITH YOU, RATHER THAN DO **REAL** WORK? SINCE WHEN DO **YOU** PLAY FAVORITES?

SINCE I DECIDED TO SEE, AFTER ALL THESE YEARS OF **SNIPING** AT EACH OTHER, IF WE **MIGHT** BE ABLE TO WORK OUT OUR DIFFERENCES.

GOOD MORNING, MISS WHITE, MISS RED. **GRAND** DAY, ISN'T IT?

BUT I DON'T **WANT** TO GO BACK TO THE FARM! I'M A **CITY** PIG!

I'D LIKE TO SEE IF IT'S AT ALL POSSIBLE FOR US TO GET BACK TO ACTING LIKE **SISTERS** AGAIN.

TOO BAD, COLIN M'LAD. YOU'RE **GOING**, AND THAT'S **THAT**.

I THOUGHT WE WERE BUDDIES, JOHNNY.

I'M TYING HIM IN **TIGHT**, MISS WHITE. HE WON'T GET LOOSE AGAIN. YOU CAN **COUNT** ON THAT.

SO THIS TRIP IS GOING TO BE LIKE ONE LONG ENCOUNTER SESSION WITH EACH OTHER? **BARING** OUR **SOULS**? AIRING OUR GRIEVANCES AND **VENTING** OUR SPLEENS? **TALKING** THINGS OUT LIKE CIVILIZED GIRLS?

SOMETHING LIKE THAT.

I'D RATHER PUSH A **MOP**.

YOU'RE READY TO GO, LADIES. SHE'S ALL GASSED UP. WATCH THE RADIATOR WATER, THOUGH. SHE OVER-HEATS.

TOO **BAD**, ROSE. YOUR **PUNISHMENT** FOR FAKING YOUR OWN **MURDER** IS WHATEVER I **DECIDE** IT IS.

GET **IN**. YOU CAN SULK JUST AS WELL ON THE ROAD.

HAVE A GOOD TIME!

THIS IS GOING TO *SUCK*.

YOU MIGHT AS WELL *TRY* TO ENJOY THIS, ROSE, BECAUSE YOU'RE *NOT* GETTING OUT OF IT. TWICE A YEAR I HAVE TO GO UPSTATE TO CHECK ON THE FABLE COMMUNITY AT THE FARM. IT'S NOT A VACATION. IT'S *WORK*. AND *YOU'RE* GOING TO HELP.

YOU CAN BE HAPPY OR MISERABLE, BUT BY *GOD* YOU'LL STILL DO THE WORK.

ALBANY

WHERE *ARE* WE?

ARE WE *THERE* YET?

PLEASE DON'T SMOKE IN HERE. I *MEAN* IT. DON'T YOU *DARE* LIGHT THAT!

TOO LATE.

MIGHT AS WELL GET **COMFORTABLE**, ROSE. IT LOOKS LIKE WE'LL BE HERE FOR AWHILE.

OH **JOY**. HOURS OF DULL WAITING FOLLOWED BY **MORE** TEDIOUS HOURS ON THE ROAD? YOU PICKED A GOOD PUNISHMENT FOR ME AFTER ALL.

PRIVATE PROPERTY

HOW MUCH LONGER UNTIL WE REACH YOUR DAMNED **FARM**?

ARE YOU **KIDDING** ME? IN ALL THE YEARS--**CENTURIES**--WE'VE LIVED HERE IN NEW YORK, YOU'VE NEVER **ONCE** BOTHERED TO VISIT THE UPSTATE COMMUNITY?

WE'VE BEEN ON THE FARM'S LAND FOR THE PAST TWENTY **MILES**.

WE LIKE TO KEEP IT **REMOTE** UP HERE, FAR AWAY FROM PRYING EYES.

OUR STRONGEST **DISTRACTION** SPELLS ARE WOVEN ONTO THIS LAND TO PREVENT THE MUNDYS FROM EVEN GETTING **CURIOUS** ABOUT THIS AREA.

CURIOUS INDEED.

WHAT ARE YOU *DOING*, SNOW?

CALM DOWN. I'M *LOOKING* FOR SOMETHING.

GATHERING *NUTS* FOR THE WINTER?

CAN'T WE JUST POUR SOME *BOTTLED WATER* DOWN THE RADIATOR AND GO? I'M BORED ENOUGH ON THE ROAD, BUT THIS IS *WORSE*.

ROSE, LOOK AT *THIS*.

PRIVATE PROPERTY

SPENT BRASS CASINGS, FROM BULLETS AND SHIT. BIG DEAL. THERE'S *GOT* TO BE ALL SORTS OF *GUN NUTS* WAY OUT HERE IN THE STICKS.

NOT HERE. *ANYWHERE* ELSE, BUT *NEVER* HERE.

THERE ARE *LOTS* MORE SHOTGUN SHELLS AND BULLET CASINGS SCATTERED IN THERE. BUT OUR PROTECTIVE SPELLS SHOULD BE KEEPING THE MUNDYS *OUT* OF OUR WOODS. AND WE'RE CLOSE ENOUGH TO THE FARM THAT ANY SHOOTING *HAD* TO BE OVERHEARD.

SO WHAT?

SO, THEY'VE GOT A DIRECT *PHONE* LINE FROM THE FARM TO MY OFFICE. WHY DIDN'T ANYONE *REPORT* THIS? COME ON. THE MOTOR SHOULD BE COOL ENOUGH NOW TO MAKE IT THE REST OF THE WAY.

MAYBE THE PIGGIES AND HORSIES DECLARED WAR ON THE DUCKIES AND MOO-COWS?

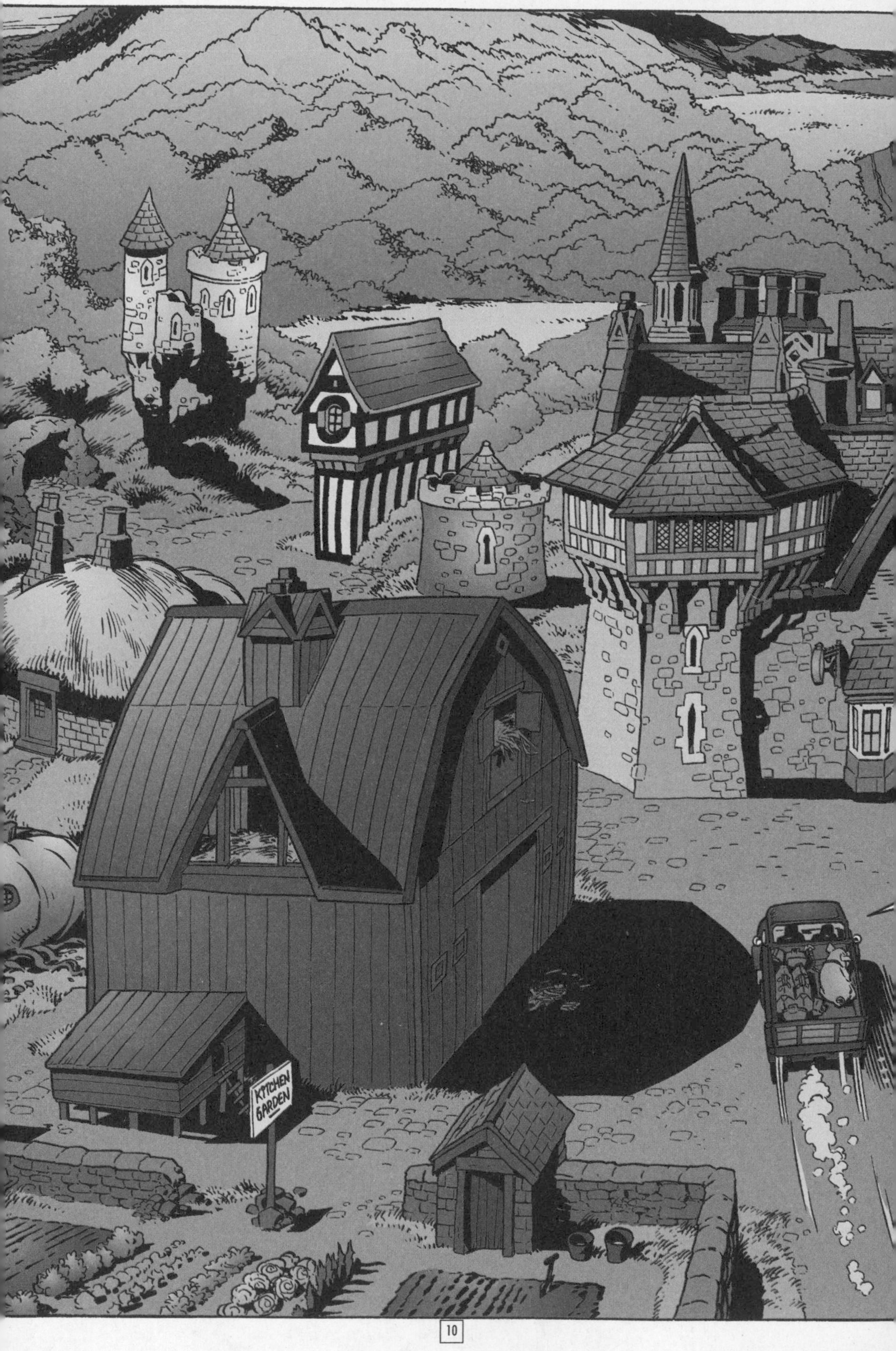
KITCHEN
GARDEN

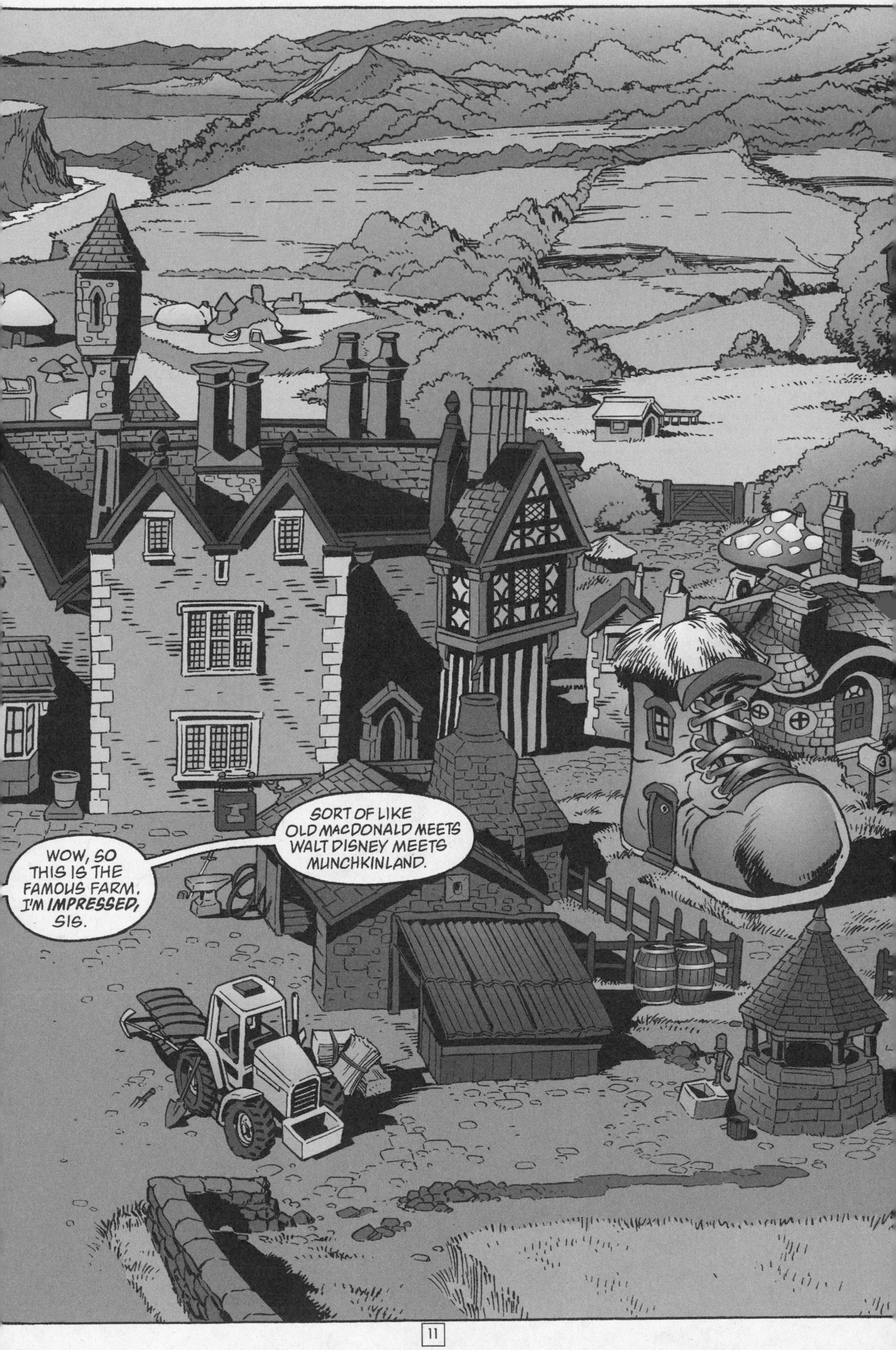
WOW, SO THIS IS THE FAMOUS FARM. I'M IMPRESSED, SIS.
SORT OF LIKE OLD MACDONALD MEETS WALT DISNEY MEETS MUNCHKINLAND.

AND IT ALSO LOOKS *DESERTED.* IS IT *SUPPOSED* TO BE A GHOST TOWN?

NO, IT *ISN'T.* HELLO!?

ARE WE *THERE* YET?

YES, COLIN, MY TRUE *LOVE,* WE ARE FINALLY "THERE YET." ONLY IT LOOKS LIKE NO ONE *ELSE* IS HERE ANYMORE.

WHADDAYA MEAN?

I'M NOT SURE. APPARENTLY, EVERYONE *HERE* LOOKS FORWARD TO MY SISTER'S VISITS AS MUCH AS *I* DO.

HELLO?! WHERE *IS* EVERYONE?

HOLD ON, I *HEAR* SOMETHING.

COME ON. I THINK I HEARD VOICES IN THE *BARN.*

IS ANYONE HOME?

AND **FURTHERMORE**, MY FELLOW **GENTLESPECIES**, I SAY TO YOU THE GREAT BARD'S ADMONITION TO "TAKE ARMS AGAINST A SEA OF TROUBLES" IS **MORE** THAN JUST A DEFT TURN OF PHRASE-- A TASTY **TIDBIT** OF ARTFUL SPEECH FROM A MASTER **WORDSMITH**. IT SHOULDN'T BE TREATED **LIGHTLY**, AS HOLLOW METAPHOR, BUT AS LITERAL **ADVICE**!

I THINK WE SHOULD **IMMEDIATELY** RESOLVE TO...

OH MY.

UH... HELLO.

AM I **INTERRUPTING** SOMETHING?

RUN AWAY! RUN AWAY! IT'S A *RAID!* THE *FEDS* ARE HERE!

I WASN'T *PART* OF THIS! I WAS *DUPED!* I'LL TURN STATE'S *EVIDENCE!*

MISS WHITE?

WHAT ARE *YOU* DOING HERE, SO *EARLY* IN THE SEASON?

I TAKE IT THIS IS A TOWN *MEETING?* IF SO, WHY IS DUN CONDUCTING IT AND NOT *WEYLAND SMITH?*

DOES SOMEONE WANT TO *EXPLAIN* WHAT'S GOING *ON* HERE?

TOWN MEETING? YES, OF *COURSE* THAT'S WHAT IT IS--ALL PERFECTLY *INNOCENT.*

I *CAN'T* DO HARD TIME! I'M TOO *DELICATE!*

SOMEONE PLEASE STRANGLE... UH, I MEAN...*SETTLE* THAT DAMNED CHICKEN DOWN!

IN HONOR OF SNOW WHITE'S SURPRISE *VISIT,* I MOVE WE *POSTPONE* THE REMAINDER OF THIS MEETING, SO THAT WE CAN ALL MAKE HER *WELCOME.*

WHY? WHAT HAVE WE GOT TO *HIDE?*

OUT OF *ORDER!*

NONSENSE! A MOTION TO ADJOURN IS *ALWAYS* IN ORDER! SO I HEREBY DECLARE US *ADJOURNED!*

MEANWHILE....

I'M SORRY, FOLKS, BUT SNOW WHITE IS *AWAY* FOR A FEW DAYS.

SO ALL APPOINTMENTS ARE *POSTPONED* UNTIL NEXT WEEK.

ANY EMERGENCIES SHOULD BE DIRECTED TO BIGBY WOLF.

WHY SHOULD WE HAVE TO *WAIT?* WHY CAN'T *YOU* HELP US?

NOW, DEAR,...

WE'RE ENTITLED TO OUR *SERVICES*, BOY BLUE.

IS A STOPPED-UP *TOILET* AN EMERGENCY?

OFFI

WE GOT *RIGHTS!*

IF EVERYTHING'S *CANCELED* THEN WHY ARE YOU OPEN-ING THE OFFICE?

I'M JUST GOING IN TO CATCH UP ON SOME *FILING*-- HONEST!

PLEASE GO HOME. WE'LL BE OPEN AGAIN NEXT WEEK.

OFFICE

≈whew!≈

WELL, BUFKIN, I SEE THAT YOU'VE *GOOFED OFF* ALL DAY. YOU DIDN'T RESTACK A SINGLE *BOOK.*

BUFKIN?

BUFKIN!

OH NO!

BUFKIN, HAVE YOU BEEN *DRINKING?*

THASH RIGH, BUBBY BOY.

DAMN IT, BUFKIN!

BAD, *BAD* MONKEY!

WHEN THE CATSH'S AWAY, USH MICE GOTTA PLAY.

♪ JUST BEFORE ♪ ♪ THE BATTLE, MOTHER-- ♪

OH DEAR GOD! *TELL* ME YOU DIDN'T DO IT!

HEE HEE HEEHEEHEE HEEHEEHEE HEEHEE!

♪ --I AM ♪ ♪ THINKING MOST ♪ ♪ OF YOU! ♪

YOU GOT THE FORSWORN KNIGHT DRUNK *AGAIN?* AFTER THE MESS *LAST* TIME?

AND JUST A BIT LATER...

YOU CAME UP **EARLY** THIS YEAR, MISS WHITE.

AND A GOOD THING I **DID**, APPARENTLY.

3 PIGS esquire

POSEY, DUN AND COLIN

3 PIGS

NOW DON'T YOU THINK IT'S ABOUT TIME YOU TOLD ME EXACTLY **WHAT** I WALKED INTO THIS AFTERNOON?

ABSOLUTELY, MISS WHITE.

LOOK AT ALL THE COZY LITTLE **PIGGY** THINGS, JUST LIKE IN A **REAL** PERSON'S HOUSE.

WE **ARE** REAL PERSONS, MISS RED.

WHAT WAS THAT **MEETING** ALL ABOUT, DUN?

WHAT **ELSE**, THIS CLOSE TO REMEMBRANCE DAY? IT WAS ABOUT HOW WE SHOULD **MARCH** BACK INTO OUR HOMELANDS AND TAKE THEM BACK FROM **THE ADVERSARY** AND HIS HELLISH MINIONS.

YOU SOUND ALMOST LIKE YOU'RE A **RETURN** ACTIVIST.

I AM. AND I'M **NOT** ASHAMED TO ADMIT IT.

I'LL BE DAMNED. AND THERE ARE *OTHERS* HERE AT THE FARM?

HUNDREDS.

A LARGE MAJORITY OF US, IN FACT.

SINCE *WHEN?*

SINCE BEFORE THERE WAS AN OFFICIAL *NAME* FOR IT.

WHY, DUN? POSEY? HOW CAN YOU SERIOUSLY *ADVOCATE* THROWING YOUR LIVES AWAY ON A SENSELESS *BID* TO RETAKE THE OLD FABLE LANDS?

BECAUSE, UNLIKE ALL OF YOU DOWN IN THE *BIG CITY*, WE DON'T LOOK *HUMAN* ENOUGH TO BLITHELY FIT IN AMONGST THE MUNDYS. WHEREAS *YOU* CAN TRAVEL THIS WHOLE WIDE WORLD, IF YOU'VE A *MIND* TO, WE'RE STUCK FOREVER AND *EVER* ON THIS ONE PATCH OF LAND.

AS LONG AS YOU *INSIST* ON THE LAWS KEEPING OUR TRUE NATURES HIDDEN FROM THE MUNDYS, WE CAN'T SET ONE *FOOT* OUTSIDE OF THIS PRISON CAMP, FOR FEAR A *TALKING* PIG OR REAL, LIVING *GIANT* WOULD LET THE CAT OUT OF THE BAG--SO TO SPEAK.

YOU'RE BOTH ACTING *RIDICULOUS*. THE FARM ISN'T A *PRISON*. IT'S A WONDERFUL, THRIVING FABLE *COMMUNITY*. NINETY CENTS OUT OF EVERY DOLLAR WE TAKE IN IS SPENT RIGHT *HERE*--TO KEEP THE FARM GOING, POSEY.

SPEND A THOUSAND TIMES MORE, SO THAT WE'RE ALL *IMMERSED* IN EVERY POSSIBLE TYPE OF *LUXURY*-- TURN THIS PLACE INTO A SYBARITE'S PARADISE-- AND IT WOULD *STILL* BE A PRISON, *BECAUSE WE AREN'T ALLOWED TO LEAVE!*

AND FOR A FABLE, A LIFE SENTENCE IS A *VERY* LONG TIME. *CENTURIES* FOR THE LEAST OF US. MILLENNIA SO FAR FOR SOME.

OKAY, *FINE*. I GUESS I CAN UNDERSTAND YOUR *SYMPATHIES*, DUN, BUT WHAT ARE YOUR SPECIFIC PLANS?

WE HAVEN'T *MADE* ANY YET. THAT WOULD VIOLATE TOO MANY OF YOUR LAWS AND REGULATIONS.

THEY'RE NOT *MY* LAWS, THEY'RE *OUR* LAWS. THEY EXIST TO KEEP US ALL SAFE.

SO FAR, WE'VE ONLY TALKED ABOUT GENERAL *POLICY*, NOT SPECIFIC *STRATEGY*.

THAT'S A *RELIEF*. IT'S LATE. ROSE AND I ARE GOING TO *BED*. WE CAN PICK THIS UP IN THE MORNING.

NO, STAY, LADIES. THE NIGHT'S STILL YOUNG.

HAVE A PLEASANT NIGHT'S REST. THE GUEST ROOM IS ALL READY FOR YOU.

THANKS, POSEY. GOOD NIGHT.

OH, BUT JUST *ONE* LAST THING.

WHERE *IS* WEYLAND SMITH?

HE LEFT.

RESIGNED.

SUDDENLY.

IT TOOK US *ALL* BY SURPRISE.

I'M SURE IT *DID*. WELL, THAT'S ANOTHER THING WE'LL HAVE TO DISCUSS TOMORROW.

COMING, ROSE?

WHAT WAS *THAT* ALL ABOUT? WHO'S WEYLAND SMITH?

MY OPPOSITE NUMBER UP HERE. THE MAN WHO RUNS THE FARM. OR WHO *USED* TO, APPARENTLY.

YOU SHOULD *KNOW* THAT. HOUR BY HOUR, I'M INCREASINGLY *HORRIFIED* BY HOW MUCH YOU *DON'T* KNOW ABOUT OUR COMMUNITY, AND HOW WILLFULLY *DETERMINED* YOU SEEM TO BE *NOT* TO KNOW IT.

I GUESS *THAT* WENT ABOUT AS WELL AS COULD BE EXPECTED.

DO YOU THINK SHE *BELIEVED* US-- ABOUT NOT MAKING SPECIFIC PLANS YET?

NOT A CHANCE. BUT SHE HASN'T GOT ANY *PROOF* OTHERWISE, AND THE "ALWAYS CORRECT AND PROPER" SNOW WHITE WON'T MAKE A MOVE BASED ONLY ON SUSPICIONS.

NOW, LET'S DEAL WITH *YOU*, COLIN.

IT'S *LATE*, COUSINS. SHOULDN'T WE GET A GOOD NIGHT'S *SLEEP* FIRST?

HOW DID YOUR MISSION IN THE CITY GO? DID YOU ACCOMPLISH THE PRIME *OBJECTIVE*?

WERE YOU ABLE TO GET A DUPLICATE KEY TO THE WOODLAND BUSINESS OFFICE?

NO, NOT *YET*.

HOW MANY FABLES DID YOU FIND WHO ARE SYMPATHETIC TO OUR CAUSE? WILL *ONE* OF THEM COME THROUGH FOR US?

UHM...WELL...YOU SEE, BIGBY KEPT ME ON A PRETTY SHORT *LEASH*, SO I WASN'T ACTUALLY *ABLE* TO DO MUCH.

ONLY ONE BED?

WE HAVE TO **SHARE** THE SAME BED?

SPACE IS AT A **PREMIUM** UP HERE, ROSE. THEY CAN'T AFFORD TO KEEP MORE THAN A SINGLE **VIP** GUEST ROOM EMPTY.

RELAX. IT'S BIG ENOUGH FOR TWO, AND IT'S NOT LIKE WE HAVEN'T SHARED A BED BEFORE.

THAT WAS IN DAYS LONG PAST, AND I'VE SINCE GROWN OUT OF THE HABIT OF SLEEPING WITH **GIRLS**-- EXCEPT FOR ONCE EVERY YEAR OR SO, AS A SPECIAL BIRTHDAY PRESENT FOR JACK.

PLEASE **SPARE** ME THE SORDID DETAILS OF YOUR SOCIAL LIFE.

RELAX, SIS. YOU'RE SAFE FROM ME. EVEN IF I **COULD** GET BEYOND THE INCEST THING, YOU'RE NOT MY TYPE.

ARE YOU **PURPOSELY** TRYING TO BE DISGUSTING NOW?

THE REASON FOR THIS TRIP, APART FROM MY SEMIANNUAL ADMINISTRATIVE DUTIES, WAS SO THAT YOU AND I COULD WORK THINGS OUT.

WHATEVER.

"HOW COULD WE HAVE BEEN SO CLOSE AND LOVING TO EACH OTHER WHEN WE WERE CHILDREN...

WILL WE BE BEST FRIENDS *ALWAYS*?

OF COURSE. FOREVER AND EVER.

"...ONLY TO END UP HATING THE VERY *SIGHT* OF EACH OTHER AS ADULTS?"

MY SISTER HAS THE WORLD'S BIGGEST *STICK* UP HER ASS!

WHEN DID IT GET SO *UGLY* BETWEEN US?

WHEN YOU CAUGHT ME IN BED WITH YOUR HUSBAND, *REMEMBER*?

OF *COURSE* I DO, BUT I THINK IT STARTED BEFORE THAT.

FOUR THINGS, SISTER DEAR. ONE: SHUT UP. TWO: TURN THE LIGHT OUT. THREE: CLOSE THE CURTAINS SO I CAN SLEEP IN TOMORROW. FOUR: I REALLY MEAN IT--*SHUT UP.*

FINE, WE CAN FINISH THIS IN THE--HEY, WHAT'S *THAT*?

WHAT'S *WHAT*?

THAT *THING* OUT THERE BY OUR TRUCK.

NEXT:
THE GUNS
—OF—
FABLETOWN!

The Story So Far:

Snow White and Rose Red haven't been getting along of late, so, at Snow's insistence, they took a trip together to upstate New York where the Fable community known as The Farm is located. Snow hoped that they could use the time away from the hustle and bustle of New York City's Fabletown to mend fences. The Farm is where all of the Fables who can't pass as human are required to live. It's a nice place, but some of the resident Fables bristle at not ever being allowed to leave. On the trip up there, Snow discovered some evidence that weird things may be going on at the Farm. And then, in the dead of their first night there, Colin, one of the Three Little Pigs, was murdered in a most horrifying manner.

TAKE THAT DISGUSTING THING DOWN, THIS MINUTE.

THE GUNS OF FABLETOWN
Part Two of Animal Farm

Written by **Bill Willingham** Pencilled by **Mark Buckingham**

Inked by **Steve Leialoha** Lettered by **Todd Klein**

Colors and Separations by **Daniel Vozzo**

Assistant Editor **Mariah Huehner** Editor **Shelly Bond**

Cover art by **James Jean**

FABLES is created by **Bill Willingham**

WHO DID THIS, DUN?

I DON'T KNOW, MISS RED.

HOW COULD YOU NOT? WE LEFT HIM SAFE AND SOUND WITH YOU AND POSEY LAST NIGHT.

I WENT TO BED *EARLY*-- RIGHT AFTER YOU LEFT. HE MUST HAVE GONE OUT AGAIN, AFTER THAT. YOU KNOW HOW *COLIN* IS--*WAS*.

HE WAS *ALWAYS* SNEAKING OUT, LOOKING FOR ADVENTURES.

I GUESS HE FOUND A *BIG* ONE.

YOU SHOULD HAVE *WATCHED* HIM THEN.

WHY? WE DON'T *DO* THAT HERE AT THE FARM. UNLIKE *YOU*, WE DON'T HAVE TO KEEP OUR DOORS LOCKED AT NIGHT, AND WE DON'T NEED SOMEONE LIKE *BIGBY WOLF* CONSTANTLY STICKING HIS *SNOUT* INTO EVERYONE'S BUSINESS.

YOU DO NOW. I'M CALLING HIM UP HERE TO *INVESTIGATE*.

NO YOU WON'T. NOT IF YOU WANT TO AVOID A *RIOT*.

A GO-BY-THE-RULES PRINCESS LIKE *YOU* WILL RECALL THAT THE UPSTATE FABLETOWN CHARTER *GUARANTEES* THAT BIGBY WOLF WILL NEVER SHOW HIS UGLY MUZZLE UP HERE. *NEVER*.

I *BELIEVE* THAT'S THE MAIN REASON YOU FOLKS HAD TO FIND SOMETHING *USEFUL* TO DO WITH HIM DOWN IN THE CITY.

SO WHAT ARE WE GOING TO DO ABOUT *THIS?*

YOU AREN'T GOING TO DO *ANYTHING,* MISS WHITE. BUT, AS THE DULY ELECTED *ADMINISTRATOR* OF THE FARM, FOLLOWING WEYLAND SMITH'S RESIGNATION, *I'LL* CONDUCT THE INVESTIGATION MYSELF, DEPUTIZING WHOMEVER I NEED TO HELP ME, *IF* AND *AS* I NEED THEM.

THAT'S NONSENSE. YOU *CAN'T* INVESTIGATE. YOU'RE DIRECTLY *INVOLVED* IN THE INCIDENT.

I'VE LEARNED ENOUGH FROM BIGBY OVER THE PAST FEW WEEKS TO RECOGNIZE THAT YOU AND POSEY PIG ARE THE CHIEF *SUSPECTS.*

YOU NEED TO WATCH YOUR *PLACE,* YOUNG MISSY.

AND WHAT EXACTLY *HAPPENED* TO WEYLAND SMITH? YOU NEVER EXPLAINED THAT.

SURE I DID. HE *QUIT.* HE WAS NEVER MUCH LOVED UP HERE AND I SUPPOSE HE FINALLY REALIZED IT.

CHOOSING SMITH, A FULLY *HUMAN*-LOOKING FABLE TO OVERSEE THE FARM, WAS AN OUTRAGEOUS *INSULT.* HE WAS A CONSTANT *REMINDER* OF HOW ALL OF YOU DOWN IN THE CITY LOOK UPON US UP HERE AS *SECOND-CLASS* CITIZENS.

DON'T BE *RIDICULOUS.* WEYLAND WAS CHOSEN SIMPLY BECAUSE HE WAS THE BEST MAN FOR THE JOB.

EXACTLY. THE BEST *MAN.* NOT THE BEST PIG, COW, GOAT OR DRAGON.

DID YOU FIND THE **REST** OF HIS BODY?

NOT YET, MISS RED, BUT WE HAVE PEOPLE OUT LOOKING.

IN THE MEANTIME, I THINK YOU AND I SHOULD HAVE A LITTLE **CHAT.**

ABOUT **WHAT?**

I COULD SENSE DURING OUR CONVERSATION LAST NIGHT, THAT YOU WERE **SYMPATHETIC** TO OUR CAUSE.

AS LONG AS THE ADVERSARY REMAINS IN CONTROL OF THE OLD LANDS, WE'LL NEVER BE SAFE, AND, ABSOLUTELY, WE'LL NEVER BE **FREE.**

I GUESS SO, POSEY, BUT WHAT CAN WE DO?

OUR LANDS WERE TAKEN FROM US BY **FORCE.** WE CAN WIN THEM BACK THE SAME **WAY.**

SNOW SAYS THAT'S IMPOSSIBLE, AND I **HATE** TO AGREE WITH HER ABOUT **ANYTHING,** BUT IN THIS CASE I HAVE TO.

WHAT CHANCE DO A BUNCH OF FARMYARD **ANIMALS,** ALONG WITH A FEW ODD GIANTS, TROLLS AND OTHER BEASTS, HAVE AGAINST THE ADVERSARY AND HIS VAST ARMIES?

WE'VE BEEN WORKING ON **EXACTLY** THAT PROBLEM, AND I BELIEVE WE'VE SOLVED IT.

COME WITH ME. I WANT TO SHOW YOU SOMETHING REALLY **COOL.**

ELSEWHERE, BUT NOT TOO FAR AWAY...

THERE, GOLDY. IS THAT *DEEP* ENOUGH?

IT'S *ADEQUATE*, POPS. I *SUPPOSE*.

NOW ALL WE NEED IS FOR MY *BOO BABY* TO SHOW UP WITH THE *REST* OF THE PIG, AND WE CAN FINISH THIS UGLY BUSINESS.

RELAX, MUMS, WE'RE HERE.

FINALLY.

THEN HURRY *UP* AND DUMP HIS *HEAD* INTO THE GRAVE BEFORE SOMEONE COMES ALONG.

WE WOULD HAVE BEEN DONE AND BACK IN OUR BEDS *HOURS* AGO, IF YOU HADN'T *INSISTED* ON PUTTING HIS HEAD ON DISPLAY.

YES, GOLDY DEAR, WAS THAT STUNT REALLY *NECESSARY*?

IT WAS *HARDLY* A STUNT, AND YES, MUMS, IT WAS *QUITE* NECESSARY. IT SYMBOLIZED THAT IT'S TIME FOR OUR *REVOLUTION* TO COME OUT OF THE SHADOWS AND BEGIN IN EARNEST.

YUCK!

NASTY!

BUT DID IT HAVE TO BE SO BLOODY AND GROSS--AND SO VERY *PUBLIC?*

ABSOLUTELY, BECAUSE NOW THERE'S NO TURNING BACK. ALL THE COWARDLY *FENCE-SITTERS* WILL FINALLY HAVE TO CHOOSE SIDES--

--OR *SUFFER* THE CONSEQUENCES.

AND, IF YOU'D DRAG YOUR HAIRY ASS INTO A *LIBRARY* ONCE IN A WHILE, YOU'D KNOW THAT THE MESSAGE I SENT--THE *WAY* I SENT IT--WAS PARTICULARLY *APT.*

WE'VE BEEN *MAROONED* ON THIS ISLAND LONG ENOUGH. ANY SAVAGERY THAT OCCURRED AS A *RESULT* IS A CONSEQUENCE OF OUR UNFAIR IMPRISONMENT.

EARTH TO GOLDILOCKS: THIS AIN'T NO *ISLAND,* BABE.

LEARN YOUR WAY AROUND THE CONCEPT OF "*METAPHOR,*" BOO.

AND YOU'RE HARDLY *STUCK* HERE LIKE US, GOLDY. YOU COULD MOVE DOWN TO THE *CITY* IF YOU LIKE.

DON'T YOU *GET* IT YET? AFTER *ALL* MY DOCTRINAL LECTURES? WHEN *ONE* OF US IS ENSLAVED, *ALL* OF US ARE.

YES, I COULD MOVE AWAY, BUT I CHOOSE TO TAKE MY STAND HERE WITH YOU. *YOUR* CAUSE IS *MY* CAUSE.

DO YOU THINK I SHARE YOUR SON'S *BED* ONLY BECAUSE IT HAPPENS TO BE "JUST RIGHT"?

NO, IT'S BECAUSE PAPA'S LI'L BOO BEAR IS *HUNG* LIKE A--

I *DO* IT BECAUSE IT'S A VITAL AND POWERFUL *POLITICAL* STATEMENT. IT SYMBOLIZES THE FACT THAT WE'RE ALL EQUAL. THERE IS NO *SUPERIOR* SPECIES. BEAR, HUMAN OR HEDGEHOG, IT CAN MAKE NO DIFFERENCE--EVEN IN OUR MOST INTIMATE LIFESTYLE CHOICES--OR WE'RE ALL *OPPRESSORS*.

OR IT COULD JUST MEAN THAT YOU'VE DEVELOPED A TASTE FOR FORBIDDEN *FRUITS*.

REYNARD!

SPECIESIST!

WHY IS IT YOU INTENSE POLITICAL TYPES *INSIST* ON LIVING ENTIRELY IN THE *SYMBOLIC* WORLD?

WHAT ARE *YOU* DOING HERE?

THE SMELL OF FRESHLY KILLED *PORK* CALLED OUT TO ME.

OH DEAR, I LEFT MY SCORECARD IN MY OTHER PANTS, BUT WASN'T POOR COLIN ON *YOUR* SIDE? WHAT HAPPENED? STARTED THE INEVITABLE FALLING-OUT PHASE OF THE GLORIOUS REVOLUTION ALREADY?

COLIN WAS **WEAK**.

HE **FAILED** IN HIS VITAL MISSION AMONG THE ENEMY. THOSE WHO AREN'T **STRONG** ENOUGH ARE NO DIFFERENT FROM OUTRIGHT **TRAITORS** TO THE CAUSE.

AND I'M AFRAID YOU'VE SEEN TOO MUCH.

YIKES!

WHAT ARE YOU **DOING**, FOOLISH GIRL?

EVERYONE WILL HEAR THE SHOT!

SO? OCCUPATIONAL GOVERNMENTS AREN'T OVERTHROWN WITH SPEECHES ALONE.

YOU LET HIM GET **AWAY**, OLD BEAR.

NOW WE'LL HAVE TO **HUNT** HIM DOWN BEFORE HE CAN **SPEAK** TO ANYONE.

ROUSE THE PROLETARIAT! **QUICKLY!**

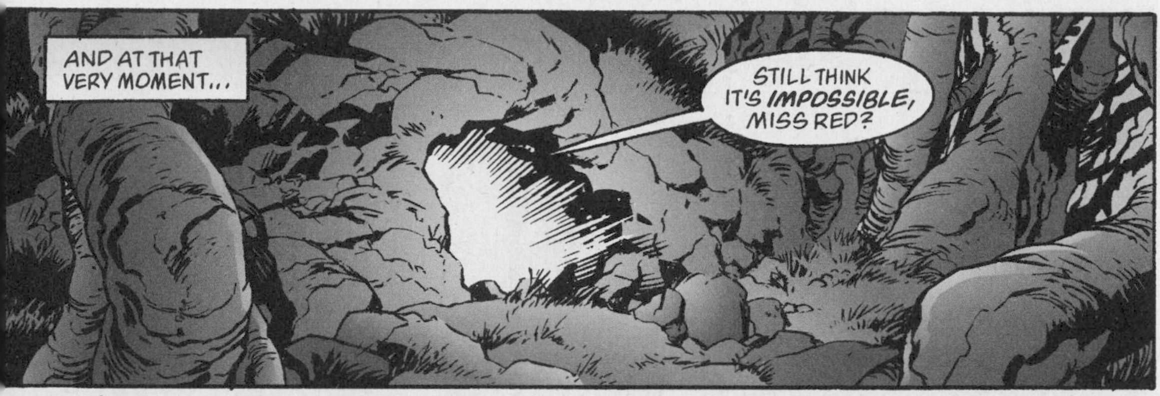
AND AT THAT VERY MOMENT...
STILL THINK IT'S *IMPOSSIBLE,* MISS RED?

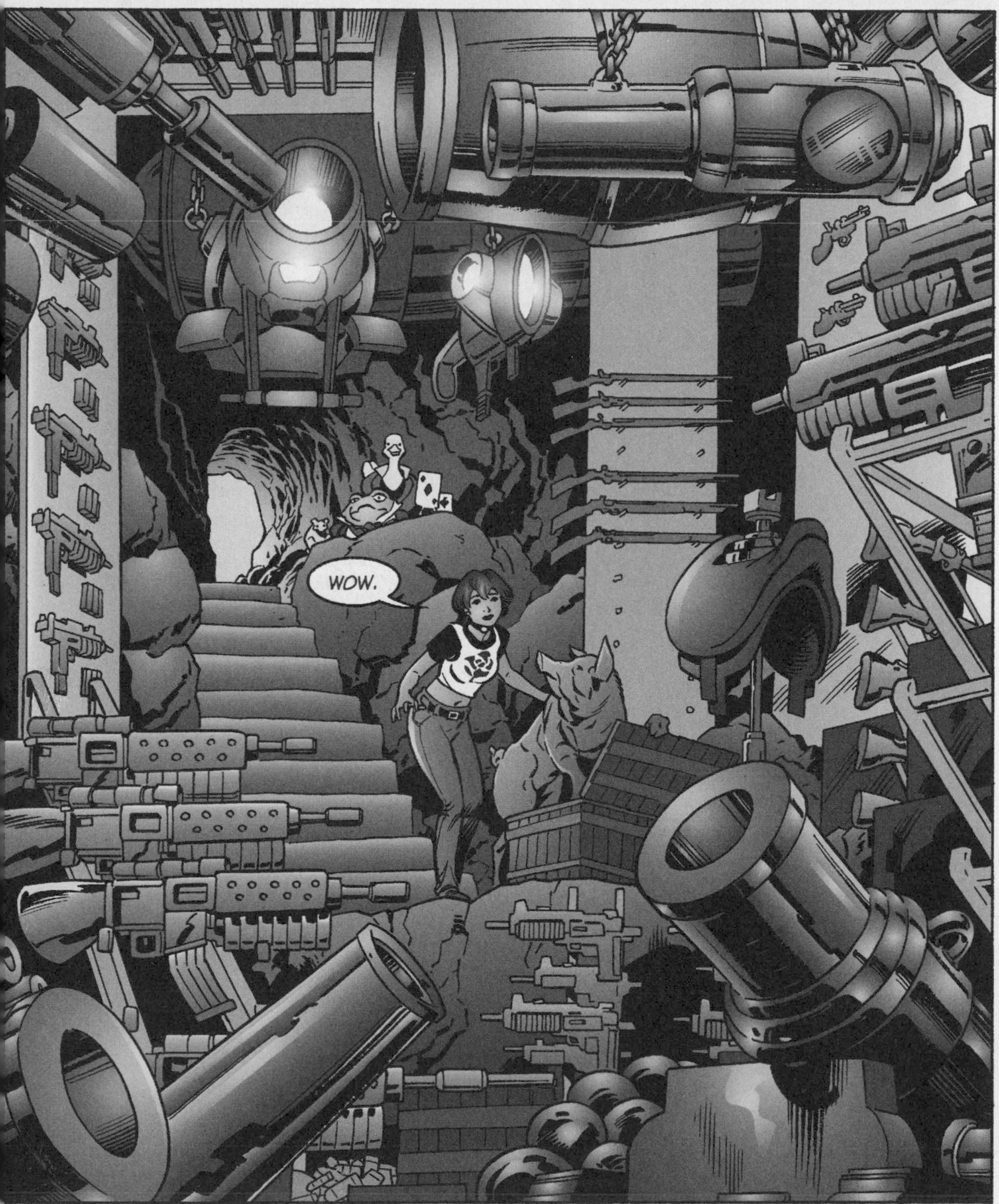
WOW.

AND A BIT LATER THAT SAME DAY...

HAS HE SOBERED UP YET?

HOW CAN YOU *TELL* WITH HIM?

WHEN I *FIND* THAT DAMNED FLYING MONKEY, I'M GOING TO--

DON'T BLAME BUFKIN. HE'S GOT THE JUDGMENT OF A--WELL, A *MONKEY*. I SHOULD HAVE KEPT A CLOSER WATCH ON HIM, BIGBY.

WELL, AT LEAST THE FORSWORN KNIGHT HASN'T STARTED *PROPHESYING* YET. AS LONG AS HE DOESN'T START ANY OF *THAT*, WE SHOULD BE OKAY, RIGHT?

and lo--

OH SHIT.

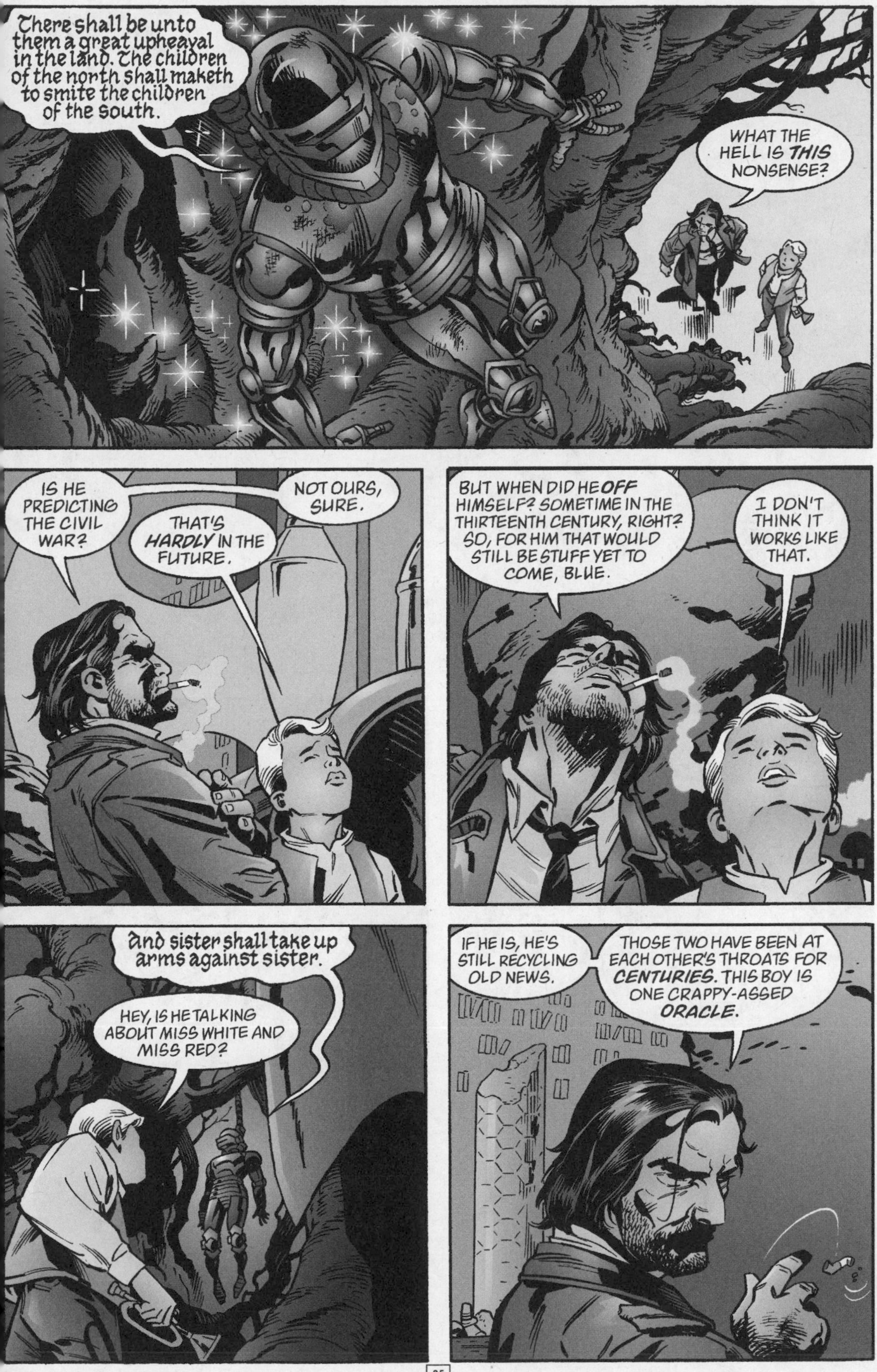
There shall be unto them a great upheaval in the land. The children of the north shall maketh to smite the children of the south.
WHAT THE HELL IS THIS NONSENSE?
IS HE PREDICTING THE CIVIL WAR?
NOT OURS, SURE.
THAT'S HARDLY IN THE FUTURE.
BUT WHEN DID HE OFF HIMSELF? SOMETIME IN THE THIRTEENTH CENTURY, RIGHT? SO, FOR HIM THAT WOULD STILL BE STUFF YET TO COME, BLUE.
I DON'T THINK IT WORKS LIKE THAT.
And sister shall take up arms against sister.
HEY, IS HE TALKING ABOUT MISS WHITE AND MISS RED?
IF HE IS, HE'S STILL RECYCLING OLD NEWS.
THOSE TWO HAVE BEEN AT EACH OTHER'S THROATS FOR CENTURIES. THIS BOY IS ONE CRAPPY-ASSED ORACLE.

AND SOON THEREAFTER...

FINALLY! *THERE* YOU ARE!

I'VE BEEN LOOKING ALL *OVER* FOR YOU. WHERE HAVE YOU *BEEN* ALL DAY?

TRUST ME, SNOW, YOU *DON'T* WANT TO KNOW.

OH, CLEVER ME. I'M A *POET.*

WHAT THE HELL *IS* IT YOU'RE LOOKING FOR?

MY KEYS.

THE *TRUCK* KEYS TO BE EXACT. I CAN'T FIND THEM *ANYWHERE.*

YOU *WON'T.*

WHAT DO YOU *MEAN* BY THAT?

TRY, FOR ONCE IN YOUR LIFE, SISTER, TO *RENT* A CLUE, IF YOU CAN'T COME BY ONE HONESTLY.

LET ME *GUESS*: YOU'RE LOOKING FOR THE TRUCK KEYS SO THAT YOU CAN *DRIVE* SOMEWHERE TO USE A *PHONE*, BECAUSE THE ONE AND ONLY PHONE DOWNSTAIRS IS AS DEAD AS A *DOORNAIL*.

YEAH, THE SERVICE IS DOWN. WITHOUT *WEYLAND* HERE TO MAKE REPAIRS, THIS WHOLE PLACE IS GOING TO HELL IN A *HANDBASKET*.

GO FIGURE. ARE YOU *REALLY* CAPABLE OF SUCH NAIVETÉ?

WILL YOU KINDLY QUIT *SNIPING* AT ME AND MAKE YOUR POINT, IF YOU *HAVE* ONE?

OKAY, HOW ABOUT *THIS*? THE PHONE IS *DEAD* BECAUSE THEY CUT THE *LINE*.

THE TRUCK KEYS ARE MISSING BECAUSE THEY *TOOK* THEM.

WHY? WHAT ON EARTH FOR?

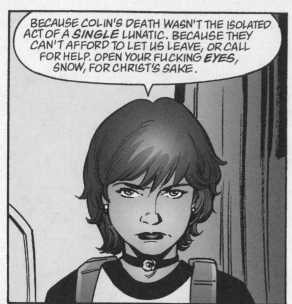

BECAUSE COLIN'S DEATH WASN'T THE ISOLATED ACT OF A *SINGLE* LUNATIC. BECAUSE THEY CAN'T AFFORD TO LET US LEAVE, OR CALL FOR HELP. OPEN YOUR FUCKING *EYES*, SNOW, FOR CHRIST'S SAKE.

ACTUALLY, *FORGET* I SAID THAT. YOU'LL PROBABLY BE SAFER THE MORE YOU *DON'T* NOTICE THINGS. DO YOURSELF A FAVOR AND CONTINUE PLAYING THE DULLARD FOR A FEW DAYS.

IT SHOULD BE RIDICULOUSLY *EASY* FOR YOU.

WHAT ARE YOU *UP* TO? WHERE ARE YOU *GOING*?

AWAY. I'LL BE GONE FOR AWHILE. AND DON'T RAISE A FUSS *LOOKING* FOR ME, EITHER.

WAIT JUST A GODDAMN *MINUTE!* COME *BACK* HERE!

CAN'T, HON. GOTTA SCOOT. PEOPLE WAITING ON ME. REMEMBER WHAT I SAID.

LET'S GO, KIDS. I'M ALL *YOURS*.

FAN OUT AND MAKE SOME *NOISE*.

BRER RABBIT, YOU TAKE YOUR GROUP *THAT* WAY, BRER BEAR, SWING AROUND AND BRING YOUR TEAM IN FROM THE OTHER SIDE. WE SHOULD BE ABLE TO CATCH HIM IN A CLASSIC *PINCER* MOVEMENT.

BASIC TACTICS.

TRY TO DRIVE HIM BACK *THIS* WAY, INTO THE OPEN FIELDS, WHERE WE CAN GET A CLEAR *SHOT* AT HIM.

DUN ISN'T *HAPPY* ABOUT THIS, GOLDY.

IF YOU HADN'T *INSISTED* ON PUTTING HIS HEAD ON DISPLAY...

WHAT'S DONE IS *DONE*, POSEY. YOU CAN'T PUT *SHIT* BACK IN A GOOSE.

YOU AND DUN ARE IN CHARGE OF THE POLITICS, AND THAT'S *FINE*.

BUT AS LONG AS MA AND PA BEAR HAVE THE EAR OF THE FARM'S MORE *PREDATORY* FABLE ELEMENT, AND *I* PULL THE STRINGS OF THE BEARS, I'M THE *MUSCLE* END OF OUR REVOLUTION.

NOW THE TIMETABLE'S IN MY HANDS.

BUT WE'RE NOT *READY!* WE'VE BARELY BEGUN THE *WEAPONS* CONVERSIONS, AND THE INVASION CAN'T GO FORWARD UNTIL THEN!

HANG THE BLOODY INVASION. I NEVER CARED ONE *WHIT* ABOUT RETAKING THE HOMELANDS.

THEN WHAT IS ALL THIS FOR? WHY ARE YOU EVEN *WITH* US, IF YOU DON'T SUPPORT--?

BECAUSE, WHEN ALL OF YOU *LEAVE* THIS WORLD ON YOUR QUIXOTIC QUEST, *SOMEONE* HAS TO BE LEFT IN CHARGE TO RULE FABLETOWN--BOTH COMMUNITIES--HERE AND IN THE CITY.

AND *YOU* PLAN TO BE THAT "SOMEONE"?

CAN YOU THINK OF ANYONE *MORE* DESERVING?

DON'T YOU TWO HAVE ANYTHING *USEFUL* TO DO? THIS IS GROWNUP TALK. GO WATCH THE TREE LINE.

GOLDY *THINKS* SHE KNOWS EVERYTHING....IF YOU WERE TO USE A FUNNEL AND ONE OF THOSE APOTHECARY'S PESTLES TO MOOSH IT *IN* WITH--

SURE, BUT YOU'D HAVE TO *SEDATE* THE GOOSE FIRST.

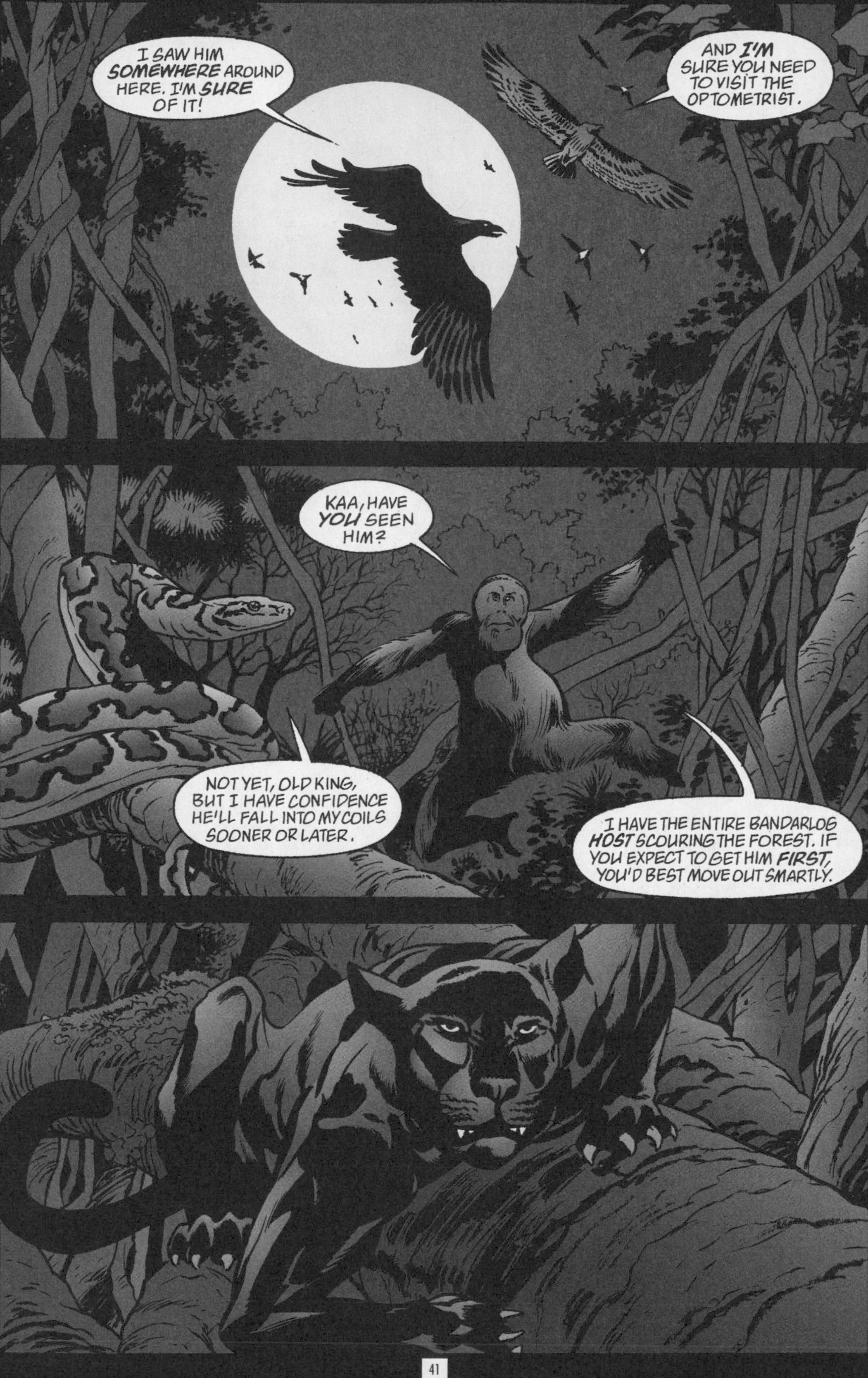
I SAW HIM SOMEWHERE AROUND HERE. I'M SURE OF IT!
AND I'M SURE YOU NEED TO VISIT THE OPTOMETRIST.
KAA, HAVE YOU SEEN HIM?
NOT YET, OLD KING, BUT I HAVE CONFIDENCE HE'LL FALL INTO MY COILS SOONER OR LATER.
I HAVE THE ENTIRE BANDARLOG HOST SCOURING THE FOREST. IF YOU EXPECT TO GET HIM FIRST, YOU'D BEST MOVE OUT SMARTLY.

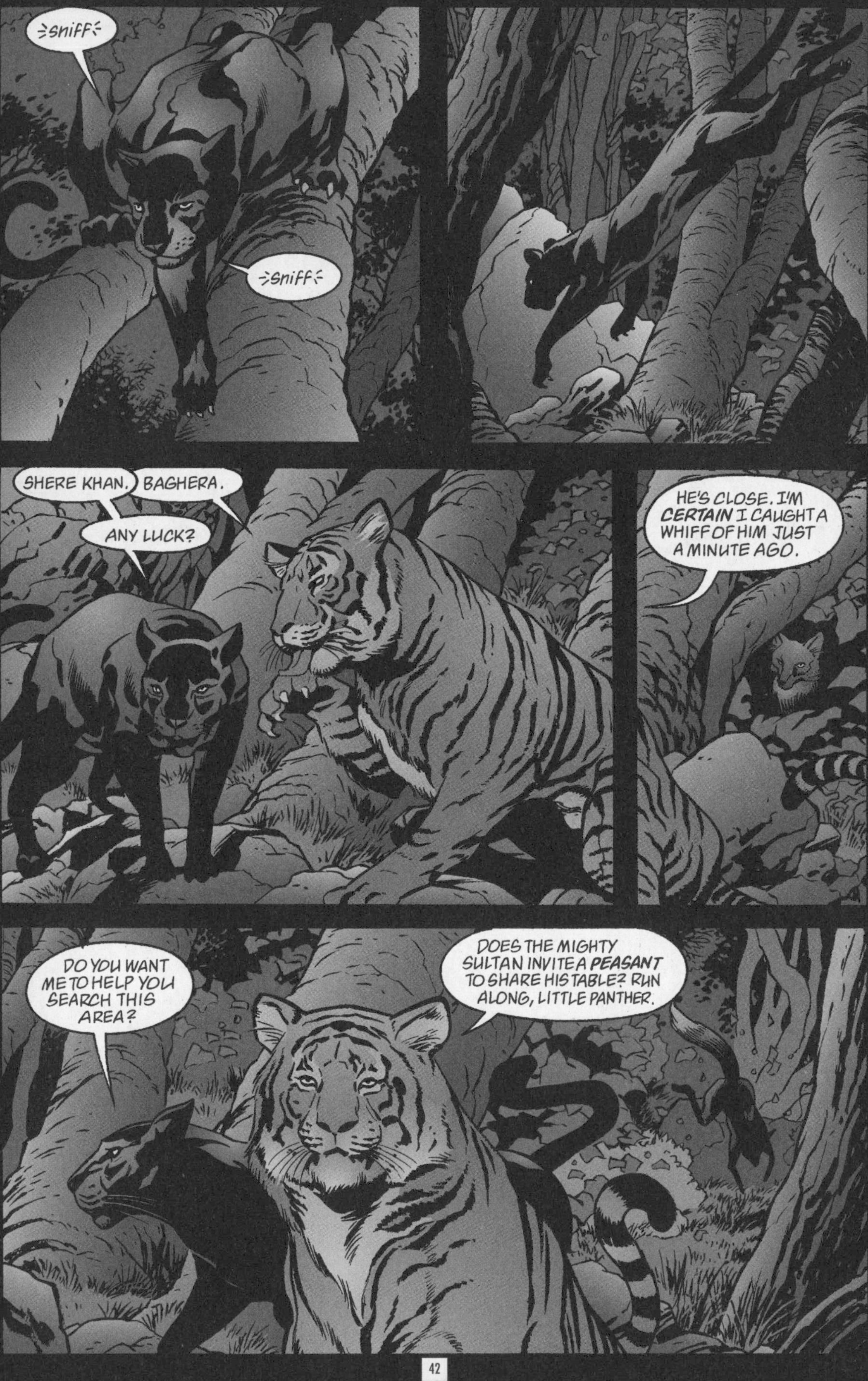

⋮SNIFF⋮
⋮SNIFF⋮
SHERE KHAN.
BAGHERA.
ANY LUCK?
HE'S CLOSE. I'M CERTAIN I CAUGHT A WHIFF OF HIM JUST A MINUTE AGO.
DO YOU WANT ME TO HELP YOU SEARCH THIS AREA?
DOES THE MIGHTY SULTAN INVITE A PEASANT TO SHARE HIS TABLE? RUN ALONG, LITTLE PANTHER.

YOWIE!

DID YOU THINK I HADN'T *NOTICED* YOU BACK THERE, REYNARD?

MOMMY!

I'LL SHOW THAT ARISTOCRATIC ASSHOLE, KHAN, A THING OR TWO.

COME *BACK* HERE!

COMING THROUGH.

DON'T MIND ME.

ROAR!

YOU DARE?

WAP!

IT'S ALMOST TOO EASY.

GATHER AROUND, CHILDREN.

THE GLORIOUS DAY HAS ARRIVED AT LAST. THE CALL HAS GONE OUT.

ARM YOURSELVES!

ALL RIGHT!

ABOUT TIME!

COOL!

SHOE SWEET SHOE

TIME TO ROCK AND *ROLL*, BABY!

BUST SOME *CARS* IN THOSE OPPRESSOR ASSES!

OKAY, 'FESS *UP.* WHO KIPED MY TEFLON-COATED MAGNUM ROUNDS?

YOU HAD THEM IN YOUR SUNDAY SCHOOL PURSE, REMEMBER?

WHAT THE *HELL* IS GOING ON?

EVERYONE'S ACTING *CRAZY*. NOTHING MAKES ANY *SENSE*.

Tap Tap Tap Tap

HUH?

SNOW, LET ME IN! *QUICK!*

REYNARD? WHAT ARE *YOU* DOING SKULKING OUTSIDE MY WINDOW?

HURRY! BEFORE SOMEONE *SEES* ME.

YOU NEED TO GET *OUT* OF HERE, GIRLY-GIRL. IT'S NO LONGER SAFE FOR YOU.

ROSE WAS SPOUTING THE SAME SORT OF CRYPTIC NONSENSE. WHAT'S GOING ON?

WE DON'T HAVE TIME. YOU HAVE TO *MOVE* IT OR *LOSE* IT, BABE. SOME OF US ARE *STILL* LOYAL TO YOU AND I NEED TO GET YOU TO *THEM*, BEFORE THE BAD GUYS GIVE UP ON HUNTING *ME* AND REMEMBER THEY'VE *YET* TO DEAL WITH *YOU*.

DON'T PACK ANYTHING. MAKE IT LOOK LIKE YOU'RE *PLANNING* TO COME BACK HERE.

NEXT: The PIRATES of UPSTATE NEW YORK

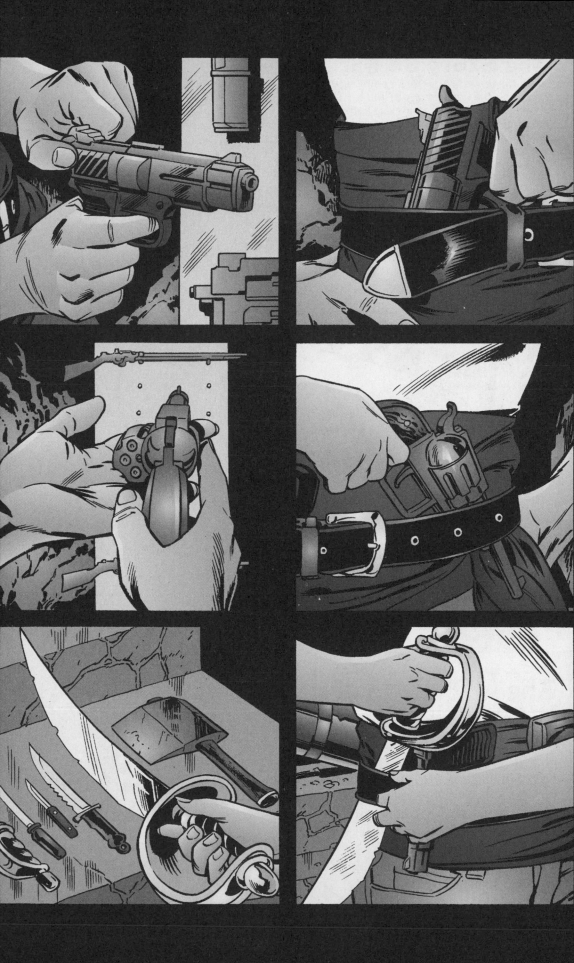

The Story So Far:

In the upstate New York community known as The Farm, many of the animals and non-human-looking Fables have been secretly plotting a revolution against the human-looking members of the New York City Fabletown. The nascent revolution came violently out in the open with the death of Colin the Pig. Reynard the Fox saw things he shouldn't have seen and is being hunted by many of the more predatory Fables. And now, according to Reynard, it looks like Snow White may be in danger as well.

GOT EVERYTHING YOU NEED, MISS RED?

THIS OUGHTTA DO ME.

LET'S GO.

IS THIS WHERE THE SHOOTING STARTS, DUN?

The Pirates of Upstate New York

Part Three of Animal Farm

Written & created by Bill Willingham

Pencilled by Mark Buckingham

Inked by Steve Leialoha

Lettered by Todd Klein

Colored and Separated by Daniel Vozzo

Cover art by James Jean

Assistant Editor Mariah Huehner

Editor Shelly Bond

FACE FACTS, KID, WE *LOST* HIM. REYNARD THE FOX SLIPPED THROUGH YOUR NET.

SO *WHAT?* HE CAN'T GET FAR. WHERE WOULD HE *GO?*

TO WARN SOMEONE. TO TELL THE LOYAL FABLES WHAT HE SAW US *DO* LAST NIGHT.

THE ONLY FABLES THAT MATTER-- THE ONLY ONES WHO COULD *STOP* US AT THIS POINT--ARE ALL DOWN IN THE CITY. AND ALL CONTACT BETWEEN HERE AND THE CITY HAS BEEN *CUT.*

WHAT IS REYNARD GOING TO DO, *RUN* ALL THE WAY THERE?

NO, BUT HE COULD SEND ONE OF THE *FLYING* FABLES WITH A MESSAGE.

DID YOU THINK OF *THAT,* GOLDY?

AS A MATTER OF FACT, I *DID,* POPS. THAT'S WHY I CALLED *THEM* HERE.

LISTEN CLEARLY, COMRADES. I WANT YOU TO ESTABLISH ABSOLUTE AIR SUPREMACY OVER OUR LANDS. TOTAL *LOCKDOWN.* NOTHING GETS IN OR OUT.

UNDER-STOOD.

ANY FLYING FABLE WHO *ATTEMPTS* TO LEAVE THE FARM WILL CEASE TO *EXIST*.

COUNT ON US.

IS THAT ABSOLUTELY *NECESSARY*? DOES OUR REVOLUTION BEGIN BY MAKING THE FARM *MORE* OF A PRISON THAN EVER BEFORE? AND ALL THIS KILLING WITHOUT *TRIALS*...

DON'T LOSE YOUR NERVE, *MUMSY* BEAR.

YOU'LL HAVE YOUR *FILL* OF SHOW TRIALS BEFORE THIS IS OVER. IN THE MEANTIME, I RE-MIND YOU ABOUT THE ADAGE CONCERNING OMELETS AND BROKEN EGGS.

THAT'S ENOUGH OF *THAT*, GOLDY. WE'VE BEEN OUT HERE FOR *HOURS* AND WE'RE ALL TIRED. THERE'S PLENTY OF TIME FOR RECRIMINATIONS AND SECOND-GUESSING LATER.

KEEP SEARCHING FOR REYNARD, BUT ROTATE YOUR HUNTERS ON AND OFF DUTY, SO THAT WE CAN ALL GET SOME *SLEEP*.

THE HUNT GOES *ON,* I SEE.

CAREFUL, SNOW. HAWK'S CIRCLING OVERHEAD.

WE SHOULD BE FINE THOUGH, AS LONG AS WE STAY UNDER COVER.

LOVELY. THE BEST WAY TO REMAIN *UNDETECTED* IS TO FIND SOMEWHERE TO CURL UP AND SLEEP.

WE CAN'T DO THAT YET, SWEETIE. THERE ARE *OTHER* THINGS IN THESE WOODS LOOKING FOR US.

"SWEETIE"?

I WISH YOU WERE PACKING *HEAT* TO PROTECT US FROM ALL OF THE LIONS AND TIGERS AND BEARS -- OH MY.

SWEETIE?

SSSSSSH! ARE YOU *TRYING* TO GET US KILLED?

WHY DON'T YOU JUST START YELLING, *"HERE WE ARE! COME EAT US!"*

SINCE *WHEN* DO YOU GET OFF CALLING ME "SWEETIE"?

EVER SINCE I DIDN'T WAKE UP BLIND AND STUPID EVERY SINGLE DAY OF MY LIFE. ANY *MORON* CAN SEE THAT YOU'RE ONE HOT BABE. AND WHO'S MORE *QUALIFIED* THAN I AM TO DECLARE YOU A TOTAL *FOX?*

AND FOR THE RECORD, I DIDN'T "GET OFF" YET, BUT ONE LIVES IN HOPE.

SHOW ME WHAT YOU DRAGGED ME *OUT* HERE TO *SHOW* ME, BEFORE I LOSE ONE OF MY *BOOTS* UP YOUR PRESUMPTUOUS *ASS.*

FINE. IT'S RIGHT THIS WAY, YOUR EXALTED *MAJESTY.*

WHAT HAPPENED?

WHAT DO YOU *THINK*?

COCK ROBIN IS *DEAD*.

≹MMMM≹

AS I'D HOPED. NO HUNTING BIRDS THIS DEEP INTO OUR LANDS. THEY'RE ALL SEARCHING THE BORDERS, ASSUMING WE'LL MAKE A *RUN* FOR IT.

SO, BACK TO OUR CONVERSATION. IN MY *OWN* DEFENSE, SINCE THE REMEMBRANCE DAY DANCE, *EVERYONE* KNOWS YOU'VE BEEN BUMPING *HEADBOARDS* WITH BIGBY WOLF.

I MOST *CERTAINLY* HAVE *NOT!*

SSSH! WE'RE *FUGITIVES*, REMEMBER? YOU *DO* KNOW WHAT THE WORD MEANS, DON'T YOU?

ONCE AGAIN, BACK TO THE SUBJECT.

IF YOU'RE ALREADY INTO BIG BAD *WOLVES*, IT'S JUST A MATTER OF TIME BEFORE YOU MOVE UP SEVERAL RUNGS ON THE *SOPHISTICATORY* LADDER TO ONE REYNARD T. FOX, ESQUIRE.

TWO THINGS: "SOPHISTICATORY" ISN'T A WORD, AND THE ONLY THING THAT'S "JUST A MATTER OF TIME" IS THAT I'M GOING TO *STRANGLE* YOU.

YEAH, SURE.

HERE WE ARE. LOOK AT THIS.

I FOUND IT LAST NIGHT, WHILE RUNNING FOR MY LIFE.

FINALLY.

WHAT IS IT?

A GUN. *SPECIFICALLY* ONE THAT'S BEEN MODIFIED FOR USE BY NON-HUMAN FABLES.

IN THIS *CASE* I SUSPECT IT'S INTENDED TO BE A *CREW-SERVED* WEAPONS SYSTEM. *STRAP* THE THING TO ONE MISTER TORTOISE, FOR BATTLEFIELD *MOBILITY,* TEAMED WITH ONE MISTER HARE FOR ACTUAL *OPERATION.*

BUT *WHY?*

ISN'T IT *OBVIOUS,* PRINCESS?

KEEP CHATTERING AWAY, TASTY MORSELS. LET ME GET CLOSE -- *REAL* CLOSE.

WHAT COULD THEY HAVE BEEN *THINKING?*

MAYBE THAT IT'S BETTER TO DIE *GLORIOUSLY* IN BATTLE, THAN TO CONTINUE TO LIVE IN -- ≷*snif*≷

--THAN TO CONTINUE TO -- ≷*snif*≷ ≷*snif*≷

LISTEN UP, HIGHNESS. YOU WANT TO FIGURE OUT WHAT'S GOING ON? THEN CONTINUE HIKING OVER THESE HILLS, DOWN THROUGH THE VALLEY OF THE BIG SLEEPERS, AND UP INTO THE HILLS BEYOND. LOOK FOR A REMOTE CAVE THERE. YOU CAN'T *MISS* IT.

WHAT'S THE MATTER?

JUST A LITTLE TIGER TROUBLE, I THINK.

--OH SHIT--

OH MY *GOD!*

RUN YOUR PRETTY *ASS* OFF, SNOW WHITE, WHILE I TRY TO DISTRACT SHERE KHAN.

WITH ANY LUCK, WE'LL MEET AGAIN, GORGEOUS.

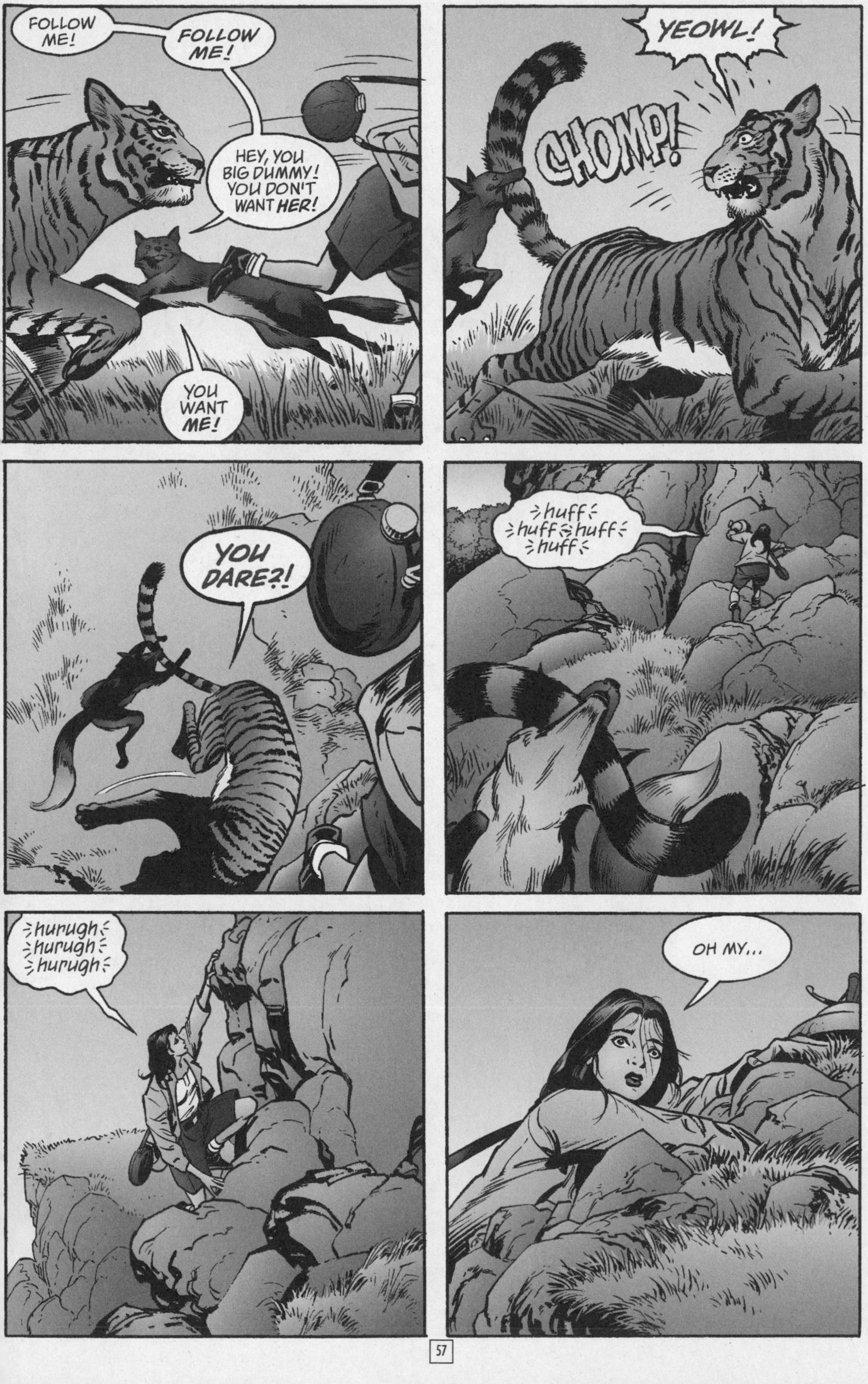
FOLLOW ME!
FOLLOW ME!
HEY, YOU BIG DUMMY! YOU DON'T WANT HER!
YOU WANT ME!
YEOWL!
CHOMP!
YOU DARE?!
huff huff huff huff
hurugh hurugh hurugh
OH MY...

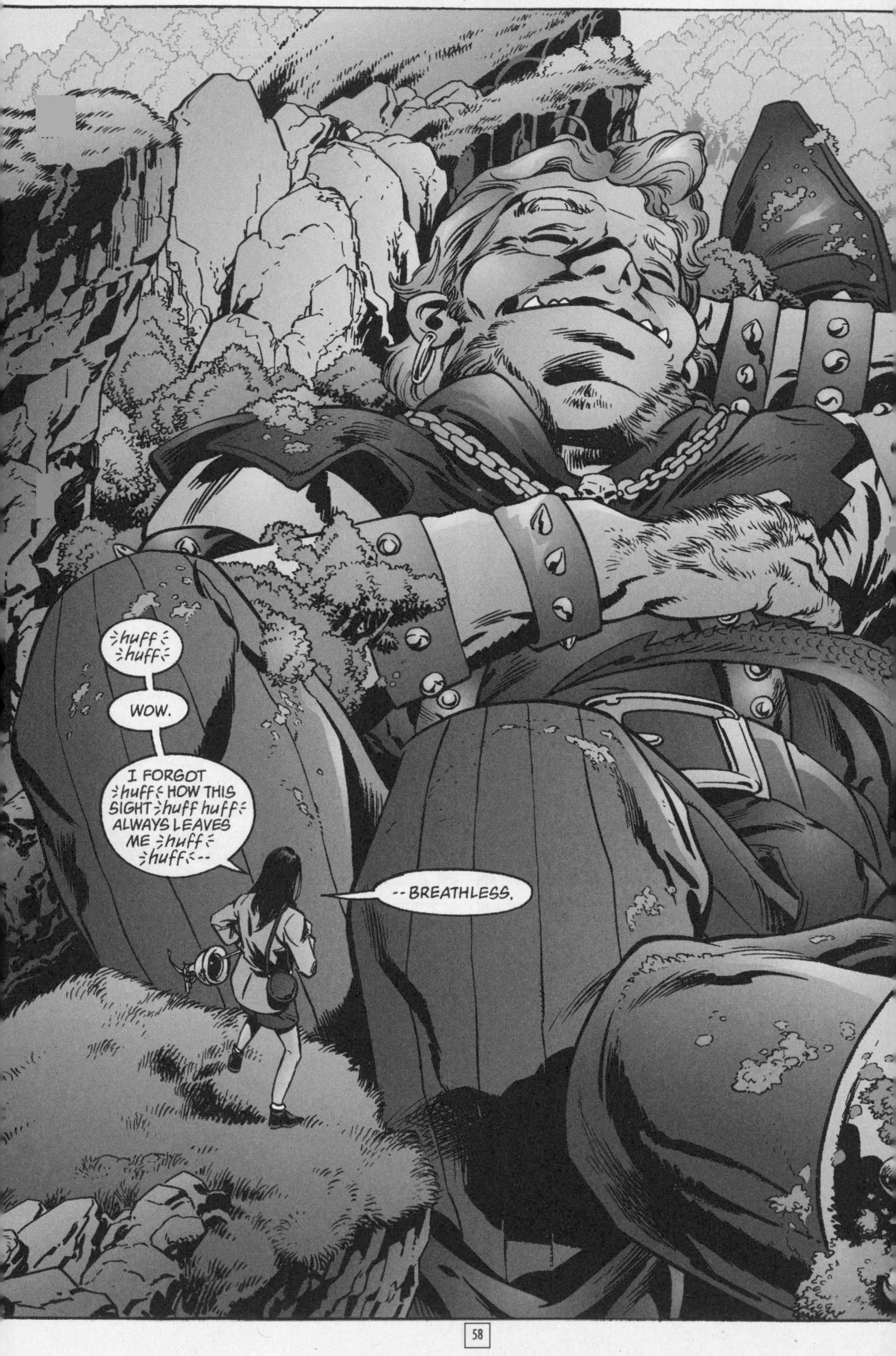
huff huff
WOW.
I FORGOT huff HOW THIS SIGHT huff huff ALWAYS LEAVES ME huff huff--
--BREATHLESS.

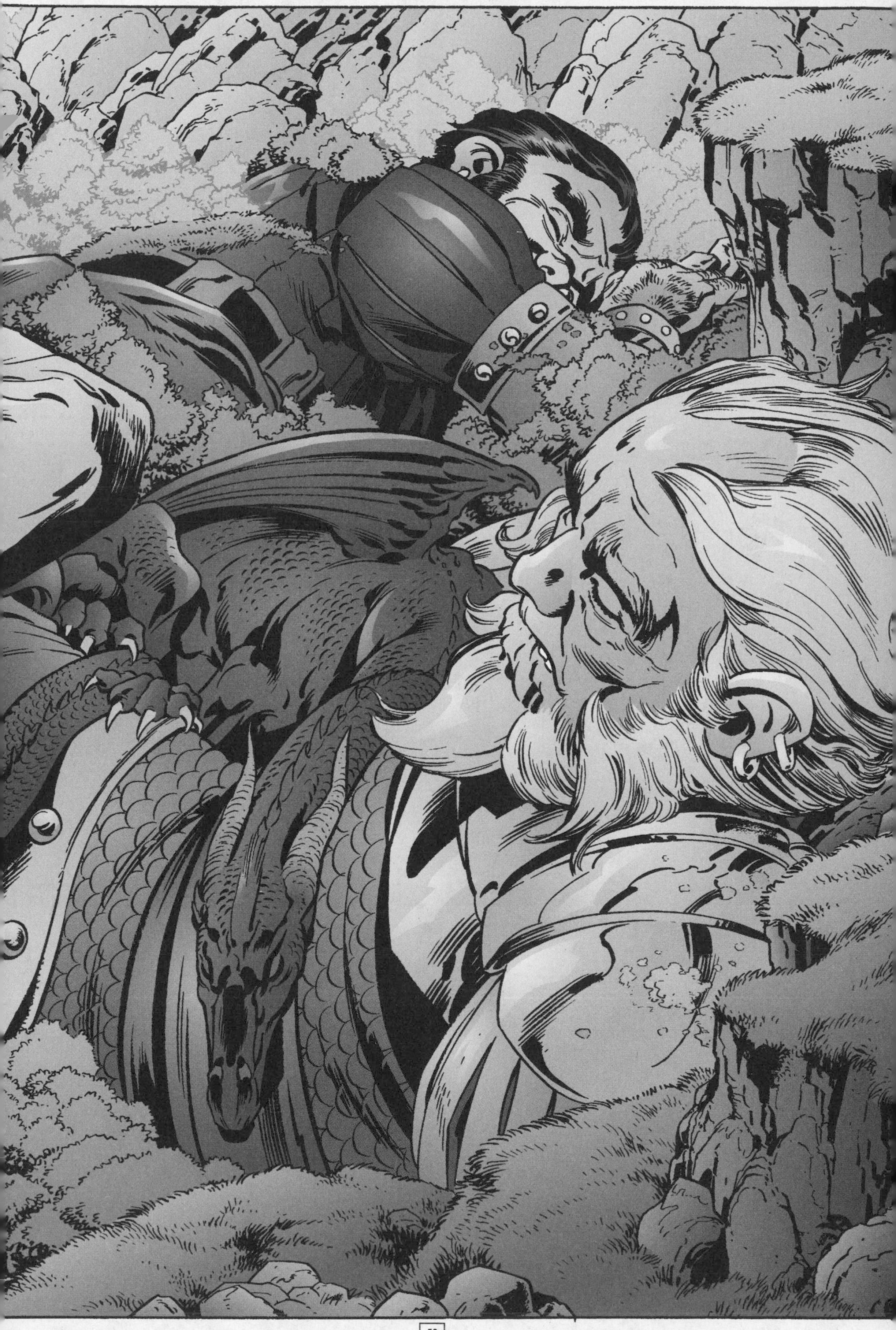

JUST THEN, IN THE BIG CITY...

OH DEAR.

BIGBY, THERE'S NO *PHONE LINE!*

AND I THINK THEY'RE IN *TROUBLE!*

COCK ROBIN IS *DEAD!*

YOU'RE BABBLING, KID.

SLOW DOWN, BLUE. TAKE A BREATH. COME BACK IN AND START OVER.

OKAY, WELL, THE DIRECT LINE CONNECTING US TO THE FARM IS *DEAD.*

SO? IT'S ALWAYS GOING OUT FOR ONE REASON OR ANOTHER.

SURE, BUT I'VE BEEN THINKING ABOUT WHAT THE FORSWORN KNIGHT SAID YESTERDAY. I'M WORRIED THAT IT ACTUALLY REFERRED TO SOMETHING *DIRE* AND *IMMINENT* INVOLVING MISS RED AND MISS WHITE.

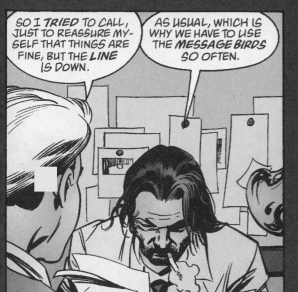

SO I *TRIED* TO CALL, JUST TO REASSURE MYSELF THAT THINGS ARE FINE, BUT THE *LINE* IS DOWN.

AS USUAL, WHICH IS WHY WE HAVE TO USE THE *MESSAGE BIRDS* SO OFTEN.

RIGHT, SO THAT WAS MY *NEXT* STEP. COCK ROBIN WAS IN THE DOCK FOR THE *NEXT FLIGHT*, AND HE'S AWFUL *RELIABLE*. BUT NOW HE'S *DEAD!* HE WAS KILLED THIS MORNING, ALMOST THE VERY *MOMENT* HE REACHED THE FARM.

HOW THE HELL DO YOU KNOW *THAT?*

I HAD THE BLACK FOREST WITCH PUT A *WATCHING* WARD ON HIM BEFORE HE LEFT.

ARE YOU OUT OF YOUR *MIND? YOU* CAN'T AUTHOR-IZE THAT EXPENSE!

I WAS *WORRIED!* AND WITH JUSTIFICATION IT SEEMS. SOMETHING *BAD* IS GOING ON UP THERE.

OKAY, KID, YOU'VE *CONVINCED* ME. SINCE I CAN'T GO UP THERE MYSELF, I'LL HELP YOU ROUND UP A POSSE.

NOW WE'RE TALKING!

AND SHORTLY THEREAFTER, HUNDREDS OF MILES DISTANT...

DID YOU HONESTLY HOPE TO ELUDE *ME*, HUMAN TIDBIT?

SHERE KHAN!

DID YOU DARE *IMAGINE* THAT SINGLE MOUTHFUL ON FOUR LEGS COULD LONG *DELAY* ME?

OH GOD!

TRUTH BE TOLD, I *NEARLY* LOST YOUR TRAIL. YOU SHOULDN'T HAVE PAUSED TO PISS BACK THERE.

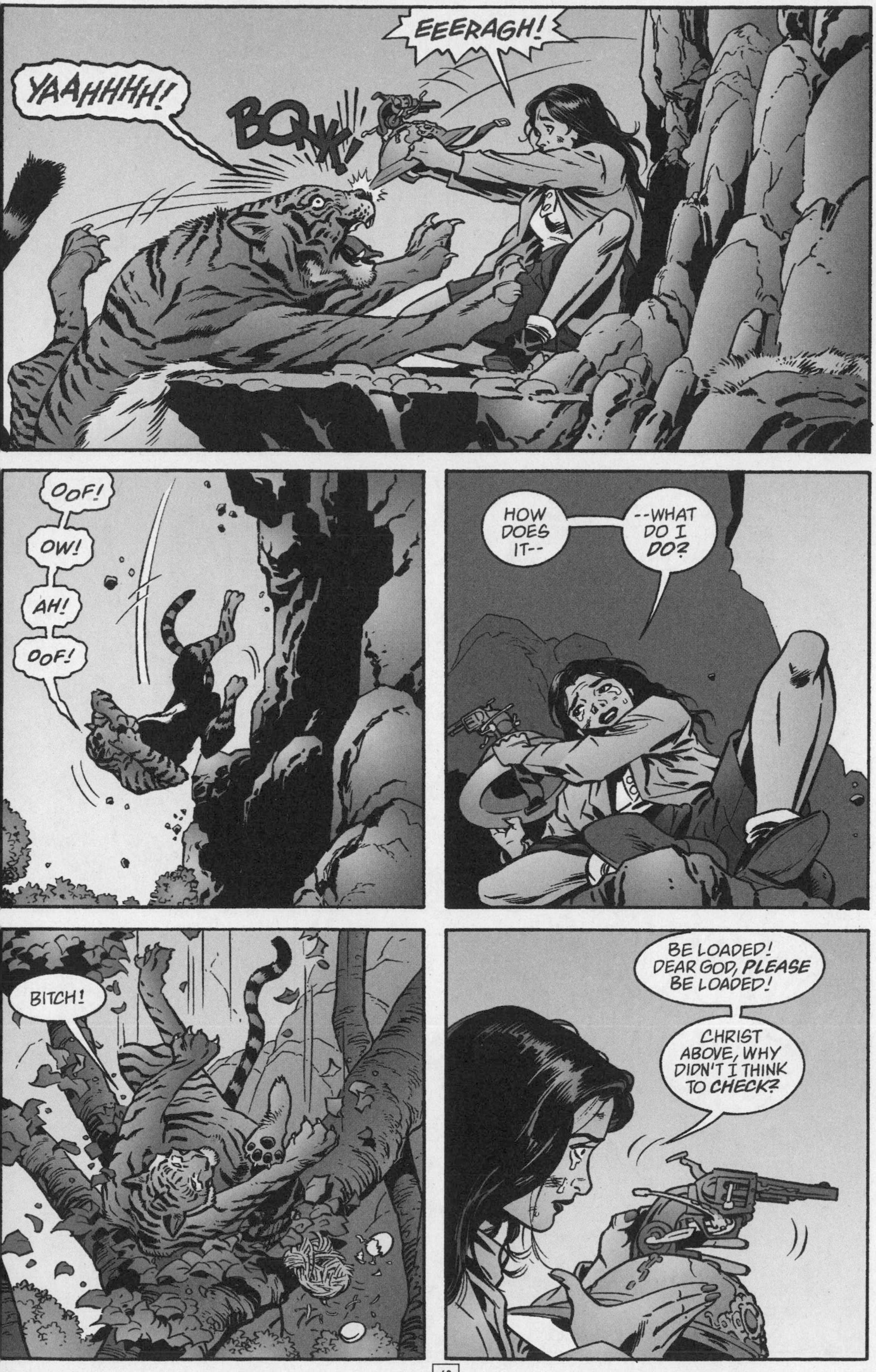
EEERAGH!
YAAHHHH!
BONK!
OOF!
OW!
AH!
OOF!
HOW DOES IT--
--WHAT DO I DO?
BITCH!
BE LOADED! DEAR GOD, PLEASE BE LOADED!
CHRIST ABOVE, WHY DIDN'T I THINK TO CHECK?

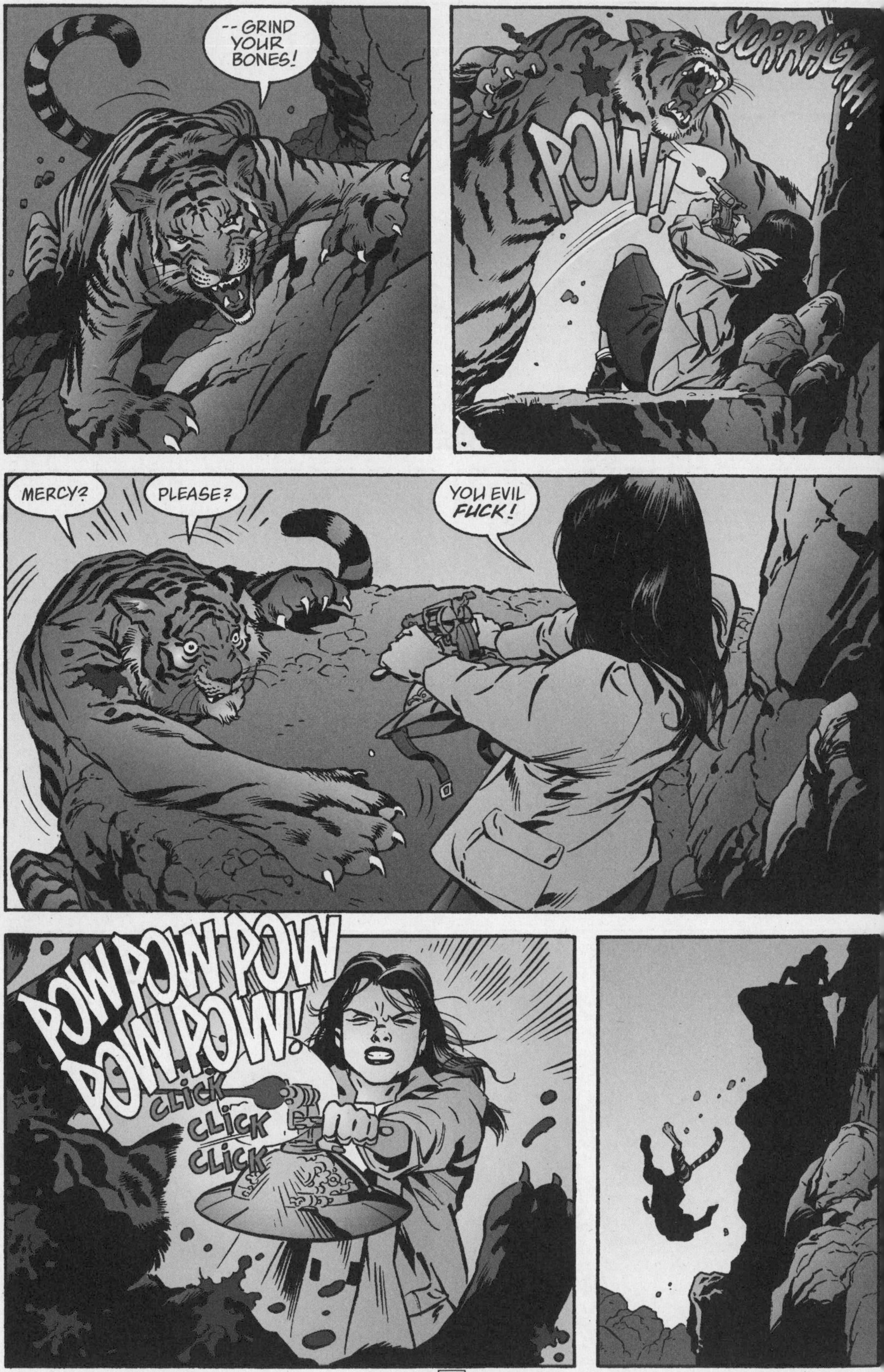
--GRIND YOUR BONES!
YORRAGH
POW!
MERCY?
PLEASE?
YOU EVIL FUCK!
POW POW POW POW POW!
CLICK
CLICK
CLICK

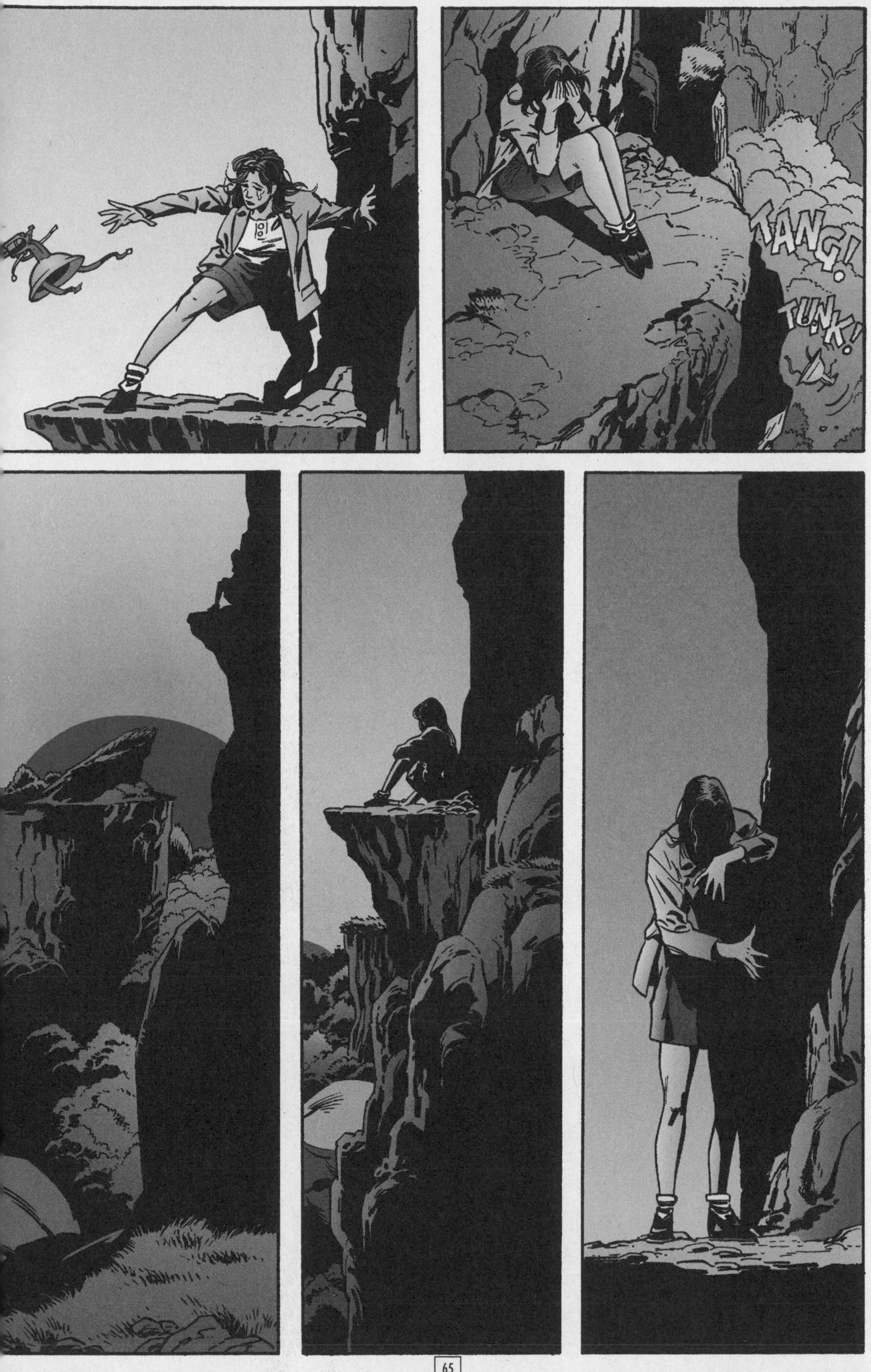
TANG!
TUNK!

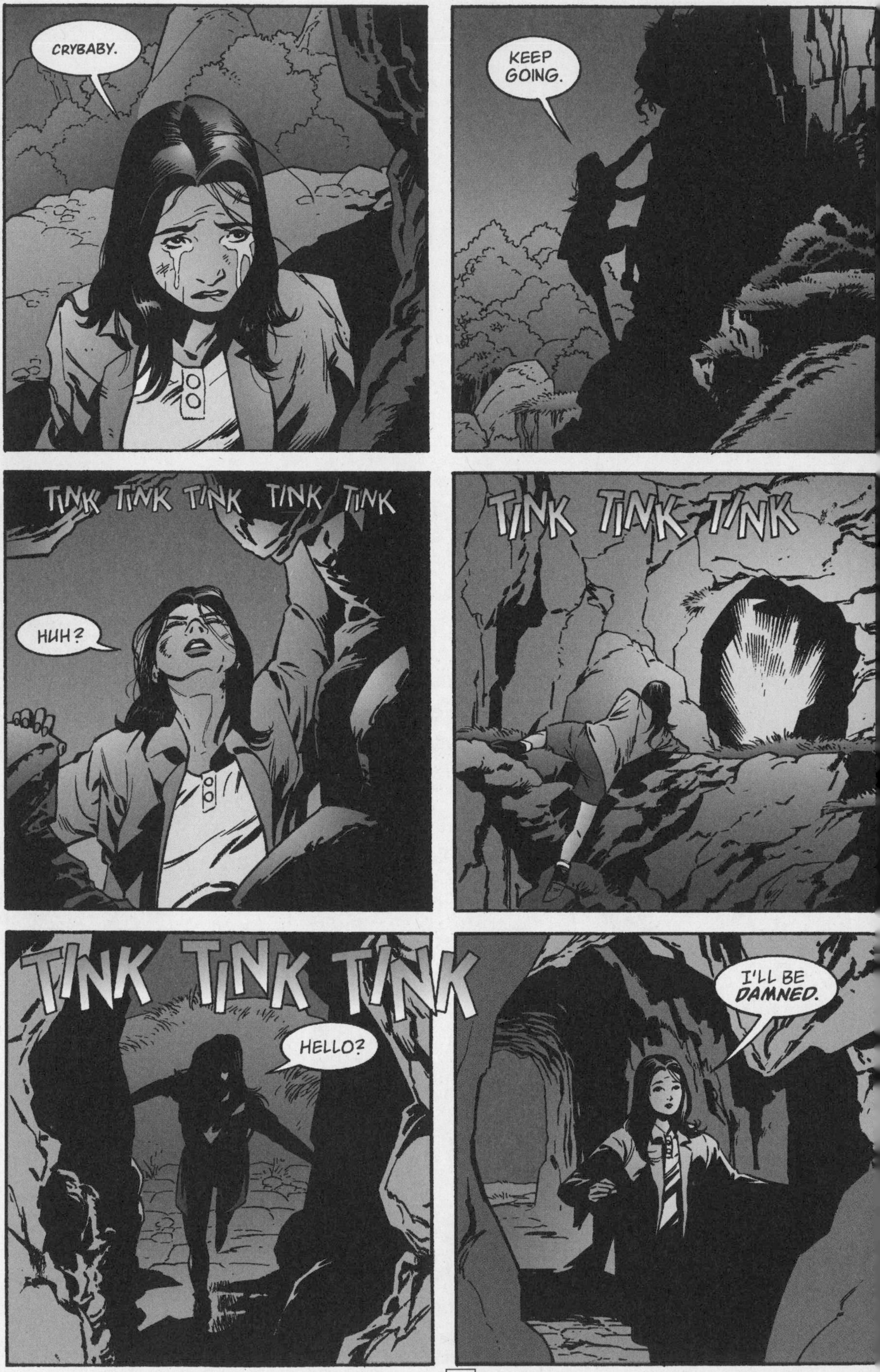
CRYBABY.
KEEP GOING.
TINK TINK TINK TINK TINK
HUH?
TINK TINK TINK
TINK TINK TINK
HELLO?
I'LL BE DAMNED.

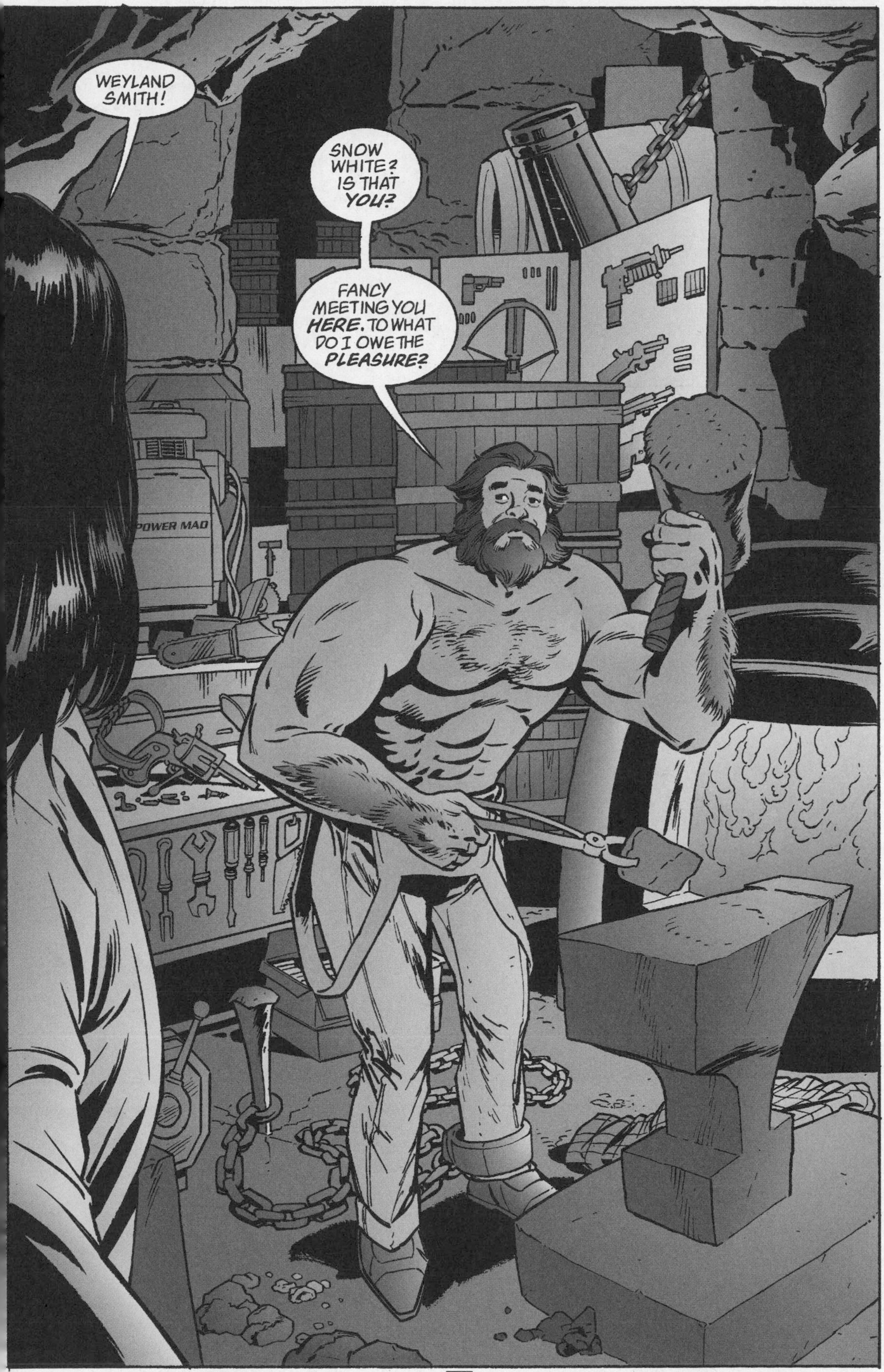
WEYLAND SMITH!
SNOW WHITE? IS THAT YOU?
FANCY MEETING YOU HERE. TO WHAT DO I OWE THE PLEASURE?
POWER MAD

WHAT ARE YOU **DOING** UP HERE? WHO **DID** THIS? WHY DID YOU QUIT THE FARM WITHOUT **TELLING** ANYONE?

I QUIT? REALLY? I CAN'T IMAGINE **WHY** I'D DO THAT, BUT IF YOU SAY SO...

BACK **AWAY** FROM THE PRISONER, SISTER!

HUH?

ROSE? WHAT THE HELL--?

YOU LED US **QUITE** THE MERRY CHASE, SIS, BUT ALL'S WELL THAT ENDS WELL, AS THEY SAY.

QUIT MAKING SPEECHES, ROSE, AND DO WHAT WE'RE HERE TO DO.

SNOW WHITE, BY ORDER OF THE RULING COUNCIL OF THE FABLES' REVOLUTIONARY AUTHORITIES, I PLACE YOU UNDER **ARREST** FOR CRIMES AGAINST FABLEKIND.

NEXT: SHOW TRIALS & PUBLIC EXECUTIONS!

The Story So Far:

Armed Revolution is sweeping through the Farm Fabletown, and Rose Red has joined the revolutionaries. Snow White, still loyal to the old order, spent all of one night and the following day on the run, in the company of Reynard the Fox. Shere Khan, the voracious Bengal tiger from the pages of The Jungle Book, tracked them cross country, quickly disposed of the fox and then tried to kill Snow. But she ended up killing Shere Khan and then went on to find the missing Weyland Smith, locked away in a remote cave, past the valley of the Big Sleepers. Just then a company of revolutionaries arrived, led by none other than Rose Red.

ROSE, WHAT THE *HELL* ARE YOU DOING?

PLACING YOU UNDER ARREST FOR CRIMES AGAINST FABLEKIND.

Warlord of the Flies

Part Four of Animal Farm

Written & created by Bill Willingham

Pencilled by Mark Buckingham

Inked by Steve Leialoha

Lettered by Todd Klein

Colored and Separated by Daniel Vozzo

Cover art by James Jean

Assistant Editor Mariah Huehner

Editor Shelly Bond

WHO SAID ANYTHING ABOUT ARRESTING HER? *SHOOT* THE OPPRESSOR!

THAT WASN'T OUR DEAL, GOLDILOCKS. MY *CONDITION* FOR JOINING YOU WAS THAT YOU LET SNOW WHITE LIVE-- *AT LEAST* LONG ENOUGH TO STAND TRIAL.

WE DON'T HAVE **TIME** FOR SHOW TRIALS NOW. AND WE CAN'T LEAVE HER FREE TO CONTINUE TO SOW HER **MISCHIEF** AMONG THE LOYALIST SCUM. PUT A BULLET IN HER **HEAD** SO WE CAN GET ON WITH OUR GLORIOUS WORK.

OR, IF YOU DON'T HAVE THE **STOMACH** FOR IT, STAND ASIDE AND **I'LL** DO IT.

FORGET IT, GIRLY. WE HAD A **DEAL.**

YES, WE DID. AND WE **STILL** DO. BUT GOLDY'S RIGHT IN THAT WE **DON'T** HAVE TIME FOR THIS NOW.

I AGREE. WE'VE YET TO CEMENT OUR CONTROL OVER THE FARM, MUCH LESS IMPLEMENT A TAKEOVER OF THE CITY FABLETOWN.

WE'LL CHAIN UP SNOW WHITE HERE, ALONGSIDE WEYLAND SMITH, AND SHE CAN HELP HIM FINISH THE WEAPONS CONVERSIONS.

EXCELLENT COMPROMISE, COMRADE DUN. WE'LL PUT HER TO WORK IN AID OF THE REVOLUTION. IF SHE DOES A GOOD JOB, WE CAN TAKE THAT INTO CONSIDERATION LATER, WHEN WE **DO** HAVE TIME TO TRY HER.

DOES THAT SUIT EVERYONE?

TANG!

MAKE SURE IT'S SET **DEEP.** IF SHE GETS AWAY AGAIN, HEADS WILL **ROLL.**

ROSE, HOW CAN YOU BE INVOLVED IN THIS?

HOW CAN I **NOT?** THE FARM FABLES' GRIEVANCES ARE AUTHENTIC, AND LONG **OVERDUE** FOR REDRESS.

"THE REVOLUTION WAS INEVITABLE, SNOW. AND, FOR ONCE, I PLAN TO BE ON THE **RIGHT** SIDE OF THINGS.

"LET'S MOVE OUT, PEOPLE. WE NEED TO PREPARE FOR THE NOON ASSEMBLY OF THE PROLETARIAT."

HOURS PASS.

LET'S GO!

CAN I DRIVE?

NO.

CAN I DRIVE?

I SAID NO!

CAN I DRIVE?

SHUT UP!

WHY CAN'T I DRIVE?

BECAUSE I'M DRIVING. BECAUSE YOU'RE A MONKEY. BECAUSE I SAID SO.

TAKE YOUR PICK.

BUT I'M A GOOD DRIVER. ASK ANYBODY.

CAN'T ANYONE SHUT HIM UP?

YOU HAVE MY PERMISSION TO TRY.

SHOOT HIM IF YOU LIKE.

THIS IS ALREADY STARTING OUT TO BE ONE SUCKY-ASSED RESCUE MISSION.

ALBANY

GOOD MORNING. HOW DID YOU SLEEP?

OKAY, I GUESS.

HOW LONG WAS I OUT?

ABOUT SIX HOURS I THINK, I'M NOT SURE. THEY DON'T LET ME HAVE A *CLOCK* IN HERE.

READY TO TELL ME WHAT HAPPENED TO YOU, WEYLAND?

THERE'S NOT MUCH *TO* TELL. I WENT TO SLEEP ONE NIGHT, IN MY BED IN THE FARMHOUSE, AND WOKE UP *CHAINED* HERE, FORCED TO CONVERT THESE WEAPONS.

FORCED *HOW?*

SOME SORT OF MAGICAL *GEAS* ATTACHED TO THE CHAIN AROUND MY ANKLE.

IT NOT ONLY PREVENTS ME FROM TRYING TO ESCAPE, BUT IT *COMPELS* ME TO DO THE WORK THEY WANT.

AND WHAT HAPPENS ONCE THEY HAVE ENOUGH GUNS CONVERTED SO THAT BUNNIES AND GOATS AND CHICKENS CAN *FIRE* THEM? THEY'LL INVADE THE HOMELANDS?

THAT WOULD BE MY GUESS.

WHAT'S THAT YOU'RE WORKING ON NOW?

I'M FASHIONING A *KEY* TO FREE YOU FROM YOUR SHACKLES.

HOW? I THOUGHT--

I CAN'T DO ANYTHING TO FREE *MYSELF*, BUT THE RESTRICTION DOESN'T COVER *YOU*.

THOSE *AMATEUR* BARNYARD SORCERERS DIDN'T THINK TO ADJUST THE SPELL PROPERLY.

THIS SHOULD DO THE TRICK.

KLIK

tdink

WONDERFUL. NOW, HOW DO WE GET YOU OUT OF **YOURS**?

I'M SORRY, BUT I CAN'T DO ANYTHING, BY WORD OR DEED, TO HELP YOU SET ME FREE.

WELL, FINE, BUT DO YOU HAVE TO ACTIVELY PREVENT **ME** FROM TRYING?

I DON'T THINK SO.

OKAY, THAT'S A START. WILL THE SPELL BE BROKEN IF I GET YOU OUT OF YOUR **OWN** CHAIN?

I'M SORRY, BUT I CAN'T DO ANYTHING, BY WORD OR DEED, TO HELP YOU SET ME FREE.

CRAP.

ALL RIGHT, HANG ON, WEYLAND.

YOU'VE GOT TO HAVE **SOMETHING** IN THIS **MESS** THAT I CAN USE TO PICK THE LOCK OR **CUT** THE DAMNED THING OFF YOU.

I HUNG ON TO SHERE KHAN'S TAIL AS LONG AS I COULD, WHICH WASN'T VERY *LONG* AT ALL.

BUT HE WASN'T INTERESTED IN *ME*. AS SOON AS HE SHOOK ME *OFF* HE WENT AFTER SNOW WHITE AGAIN.

DID HE *SUCCEED?* IS SHE *DEAD?*

I DON'T KNOW, KING NOBLE. MY DAILY *RATION* OF BRAVERY WAS ALREADY USED UP BY TRYING TO DISTRACT KHAN IN THE FIRST PLACE. AFTER THAT, WHEN THE TIGER WENT IN *ONE* DIRECTION, I THOUGHT IT PRUDENT TO GO IN THE *OTHER*.

HOW MANY OF US REMAIN LOYAL?

NOT MANY. THE BR'ER GROUP AND THE JUNGLE GROUP ARE WITH THE OTHER SIDE, ALONG WITH A FEW ASSORTED OTHERS, BUT THE MAJORITY IS STILL STRADDLING THE *FENCE,* WAITING TO SEE HOW IT ALL SHAKES OUT.

TRY TO FIND SNOW WHITE AGAIN. IF SHE'S *ALIVE,* WE'LL HANG ON. IF NOT, THE BEST WE CAN DO IS TO TRY TO ESCAPE THESE LANDS DURING THEIR MIDDAY RALLY.

NOT MUCH OF A *PLAN,* BUT IF THAT'S ALL WE'VE GOT...

OPEN *UP*, IN THE NAME OF THE REVOLU-TION!

WHAT DO YOU *WANT*, BR'ER RABBIT? WHY ALL THIS POUNDING ON MY DOOR?

GOOD MORNING, BILL. THE GRAND REVOLUTIONARY AUTHOR-ITY INVITES YOU TO TAKE PART IN A BIG RALLY IN THE VILLAGE CENTER AT NOON.

ATTENDANCE IS *MANDATORY*.

BILLY GOATS GRUFF

OPEN *UP*, TOM THUMB, IN THE NAME OF THE REVOLUTION!

MAYBE HE'S OVER AT MISS THUMBELINA'S HOUSE AGAIN. I HEARD THEY WERE BACK TOGETHER.

SO, SNOW WHITE *WASN'T* AS HELPLESS AS SHE LOOKED.

GOOD FOR HER.

OUCH! ARE YOU TRYING TO TAKE MY *LEG* OFF?

SORRY. I'VE NEVER BEEN HANDY WITH TOOLS.

IT WOULD HELP IF THAT *SPELL* DIDN'T KEEP MAKING YOU FLINCH.

THAT HAS *NOTHING* TO DO WITH THE SPELL AND *EVERY-THING* TO DO WITH SIMPLE SELF-PRESERVATION.

GIVE ME A *BREAK*. I'M DOING THE BEST I CAN.

OKAY-- THIS ISN'T WORKING. I GIVE UP. WHY DON'T I LOOK FOR SOMETHING I CAN TRY TO *PICK* THE LOCK WITH?

I'M SORRY, BUT I CAN'T DO--

YEAH, I KNOW. SHUT UP.

WHY DON'T YOU TRY THIS *KEY* LYING HERE?

HUH?

OR HAVE YOU ALREADY *TRIED* IT, SNOW BUNNY?

REYNARD. I WAS *WONDERING* WHEN YOU'D SHOW UP.

THAT KEY WAS THE ONE WEYLAND MADE TO UNFASTEN *MY* SHACKLES. IT WON'T WORK ON HIS.

WHY NOT? THE *LOCKS* LOOK THE SAME.

UHM.... WELL.... I DON'T KNOW.

DO YOU THINK THIS COULD WORK ON YOURS, TOO?

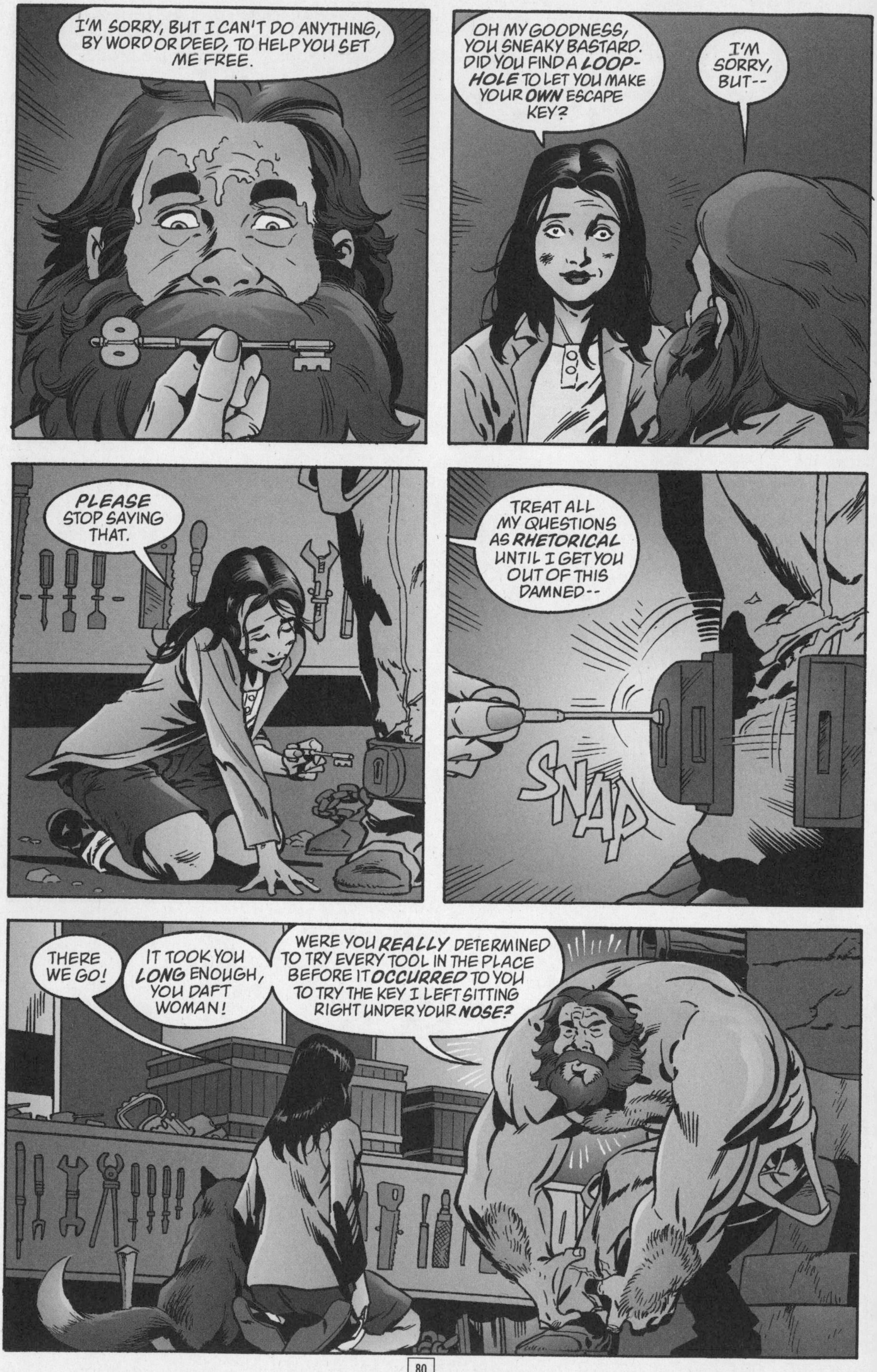
I'M SORRY, BUT I CAN'T DO ANYTHING, BY WORD OR DEED, TO HELP YOU SET ME FREE.
OH MY GOODNESS, YOU SNEAKY BASTARD. DID YOU FIND A LOOP-HOLE TO LET YOU MAKE YOUR OWN ESCAPE KEY?
I'M SORRY, BUT--
PLEASE STOP SAYING THAT.
TREAT ALL MY QUESTIONS AS RHETORICAL UNTIL I GET YOU OUT OF THIS DAMNED--
SNAP
THERE WE GO!
IT TOOK YOU LONG ENOUGH, YOU DAFT WOMAN!
WERE YOU REALLY DETERMINED TO TRY EVERY TOOL IN THE PLACE BEFORE IT OCCURRED TO YOU TO TRY THE KEY I LEFT SITTING RIGHT UNDER YOUR NOSE?

YOU'RE ALLOWED **ONE** RUDE COMMENT DUE TO THE OBVIOUS FRUSTRATIONS OF BEING CAPTIVE FOR SO LONG. BUT DON'T **PUSH** IT.

KIDS, THIS REALLY ISN'T THE BEST TIME TO ARGUE.

THE FOX IS RIGHT. WE NEED TO MOVE FAST, BEFORE THIS RIDICULOUS ANIMAL REVOLUTION GOES ANY FURTHER.

YOU HAVE A PLAN, PRINCESS?

POSSIBLY.

WEYLAND, CAN YOU ANSWER QUESTIONS NOW?

YES.

THEN I NEED TO KNOW THREE THINGS. FIRST, HOW MANY WORKING GUNS DO THESE IDIOTS HAVE SO FAR?

PLENTY. EVERY FABLE WHO COULD USE UNMODIFIED GUNS ALREADY HAS ONE.

WHAT ABOUT ADVANCED COMMUNICATIONS? WHAT DO THEY HAVE AND WHAT DO YOU HAVE HERE TO WORK WITH?

THEY DON'T HAVE MUCH OF ANYTHING YET. LIKE AMATEUR SOLDIERS THROUGHOUT HISTORY, THEY MADE THE MISTAKE OF PUTTING WEAPONS ACQUISITION *BEFORE* COMMUNICATIONS.

WE'VE GOT ALL SORTS OF ELECTRONICS HERE, WHICH I WAS INSTRUCTED TO START MODIFYING ONLY *AFTER* I COMPLETED ALL THE GUNS. WHAT DO YOU NEED?

WE'LL GET TO THAT. NEXT, TELL ME ABOUT THE BIG SLEEPERS. WHY DO THEY *SLEEP* FOR SO LONG?

ARE YOU ASKING ME WHAT SPELLS CAUSE THEM TO *REMAIN* ASLEEP, OR WHY IT'S IN OUR INTEREST TO *KEEP* SUCH IMPOSSIBLE-TO-EXPLAIN CREATURES ASLEEP AND OUT OF SIGHT?

"NEITHER, REALLY. I'M ASKING WHAT IT WILL TAKE TO *WAKE* THEM."

"REYNARD, I NEED YOU TO SNEAK BACK INTO THE VILLAGE AS QUICKLY AS POSSIBLE, AND PASS THE WORD. FOR THEIR *OWN* GOOD, ANY FABLE STILL LOYAL TO US BETTER BE OUT OF TOWN BY THE BIG NOON RALLY."

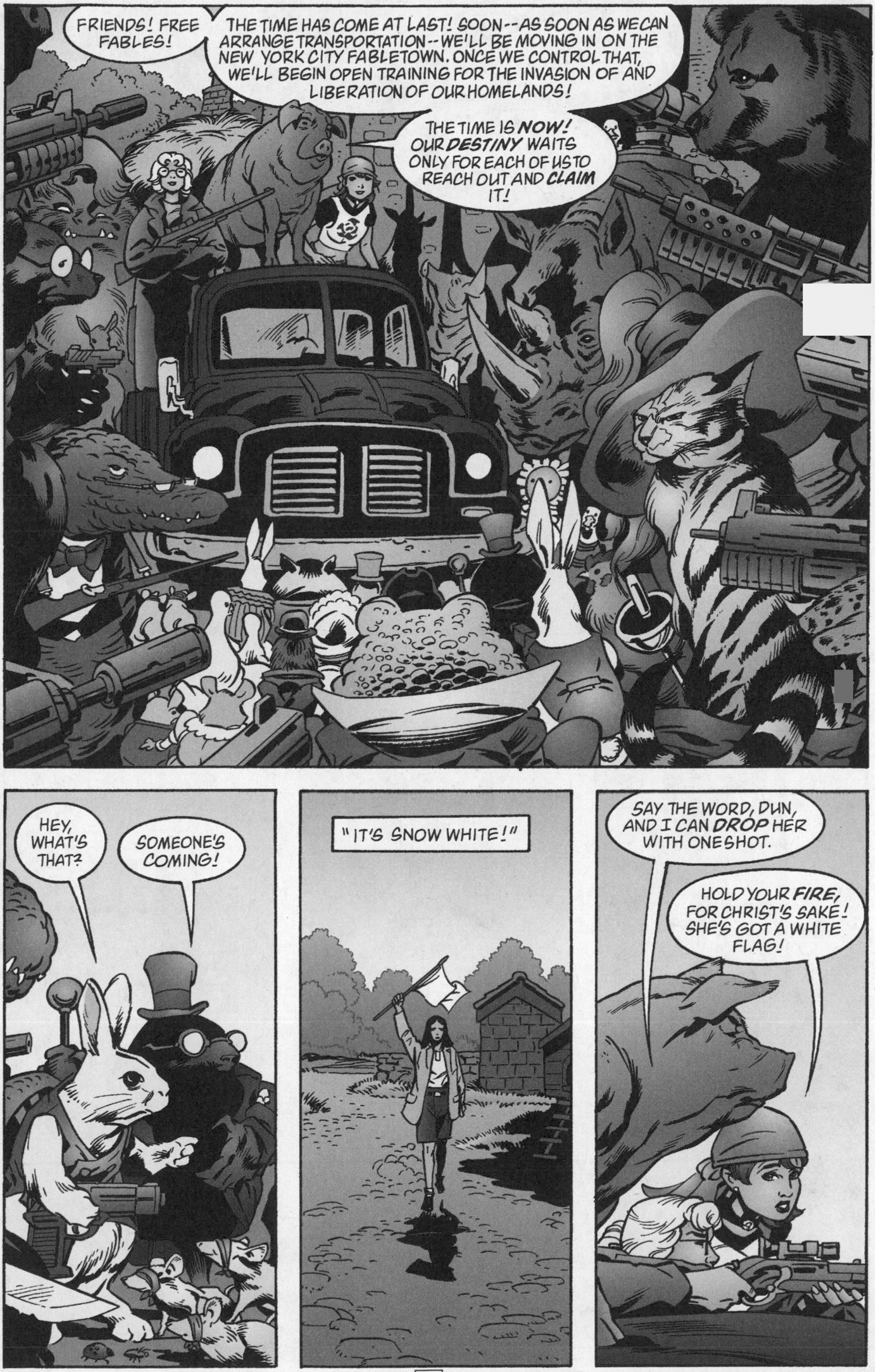
FRIENDS! FREE FABLES!
THE TIME HAS COME AT LAST! SOON--AS SOON AS WE CAN ARRANGE TRANSPORTATION--WE'LL BE MOVING IN ON THE NEW YORK CITY FABLETOWN. ONCE WE CONTROL THAT, WE'LL BEGIN OPEN TRAINING FOR THE INVASION OF AND LIBERATION OF OUR HOMELANDS!
THE TIME IS NOW! OUR DESTINY WAITS ONLY FOR EACH OF US TO REACH OUT AND CLAIM IT!
HEY, WHAT'S THAT?
SOMEONE'S COMING!
"IT'S SNOW WHITE!"
SAY THE WORD, DUN, AND I CAN DROP HER WITH ONE SHOT.
HOLD YOUR FIRE, FOR CHRIST'S SAKE! SHE'S GOT A WHITE FLAG!

EVERYONE DROP YOUR GUNS AND DISPERSE!

YOUR SO-CALLED *REVOLUTION* IS OVER!

WHAT?

WHY *SHOULD* WE?

BUT WE'VE GOT YOU *OUTGUNNED!*

YOU DUMB *BASTARDS!* I'M SNOW WHITE! I *RUN* FABLETOWN AND I'M *NEVER* OUTGUNNED!

KILL THE BARN.

OH MY GOD!

WE'RE *FUCKED!*

IF ANYTHING HAPPENS TO ME, *BURN* THE TOWN, EVERYONE IN IT, AND ANYONE WHO TRIES TO *ESCAPE.*

WHAT DO WE *DO?*

WHAT *CAN* WE DO? MY SISTER *SKUNKED* US!

MOVE THE BROTHERS IN, *NOW.*

THEY'RE ALREADY ON THE WAY!

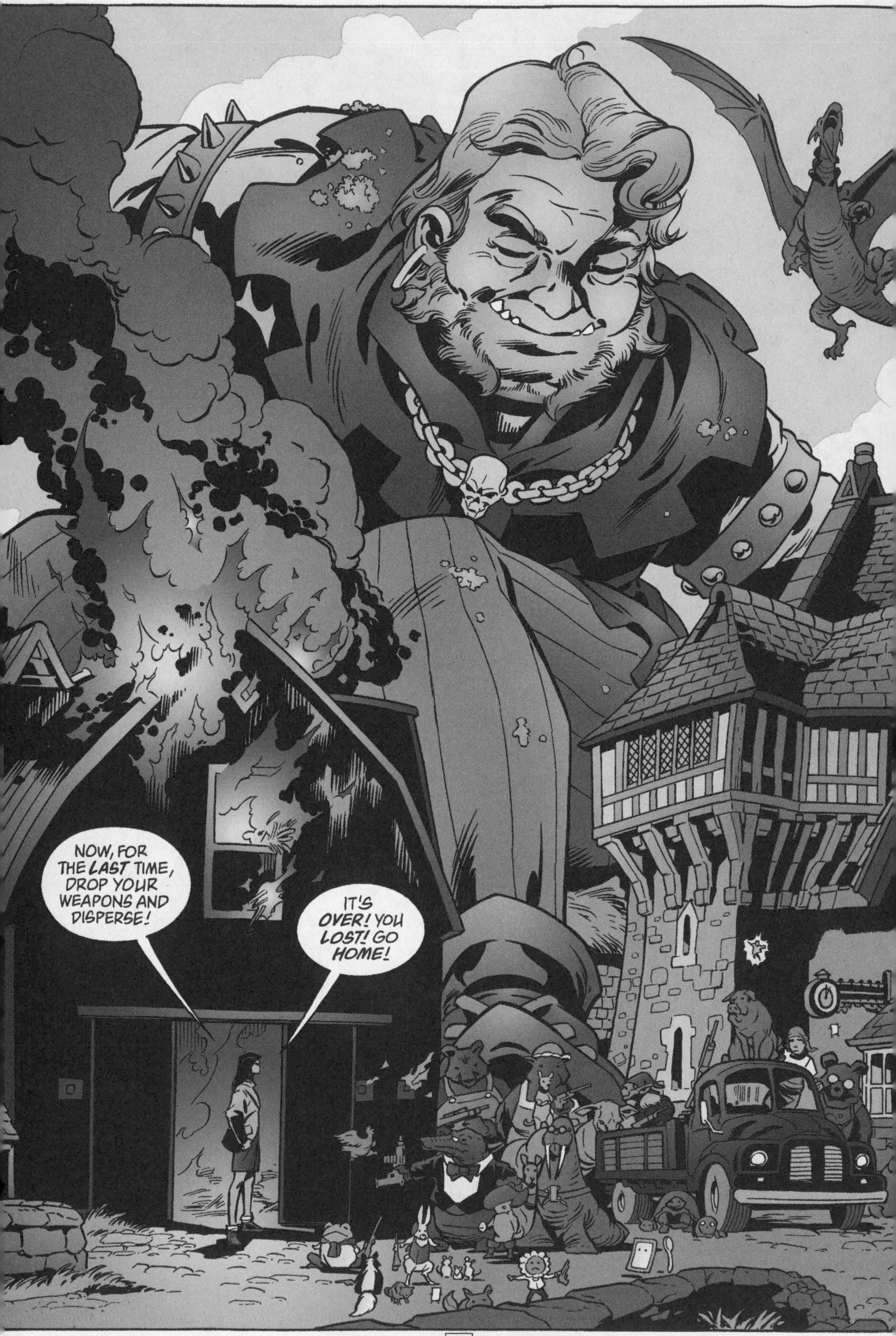
NOW, FOR THE LAST TIME, DROP YOUR WEAPONS AND DISPERSE!
IT'S OVER! YOU LOST! GO HOME!

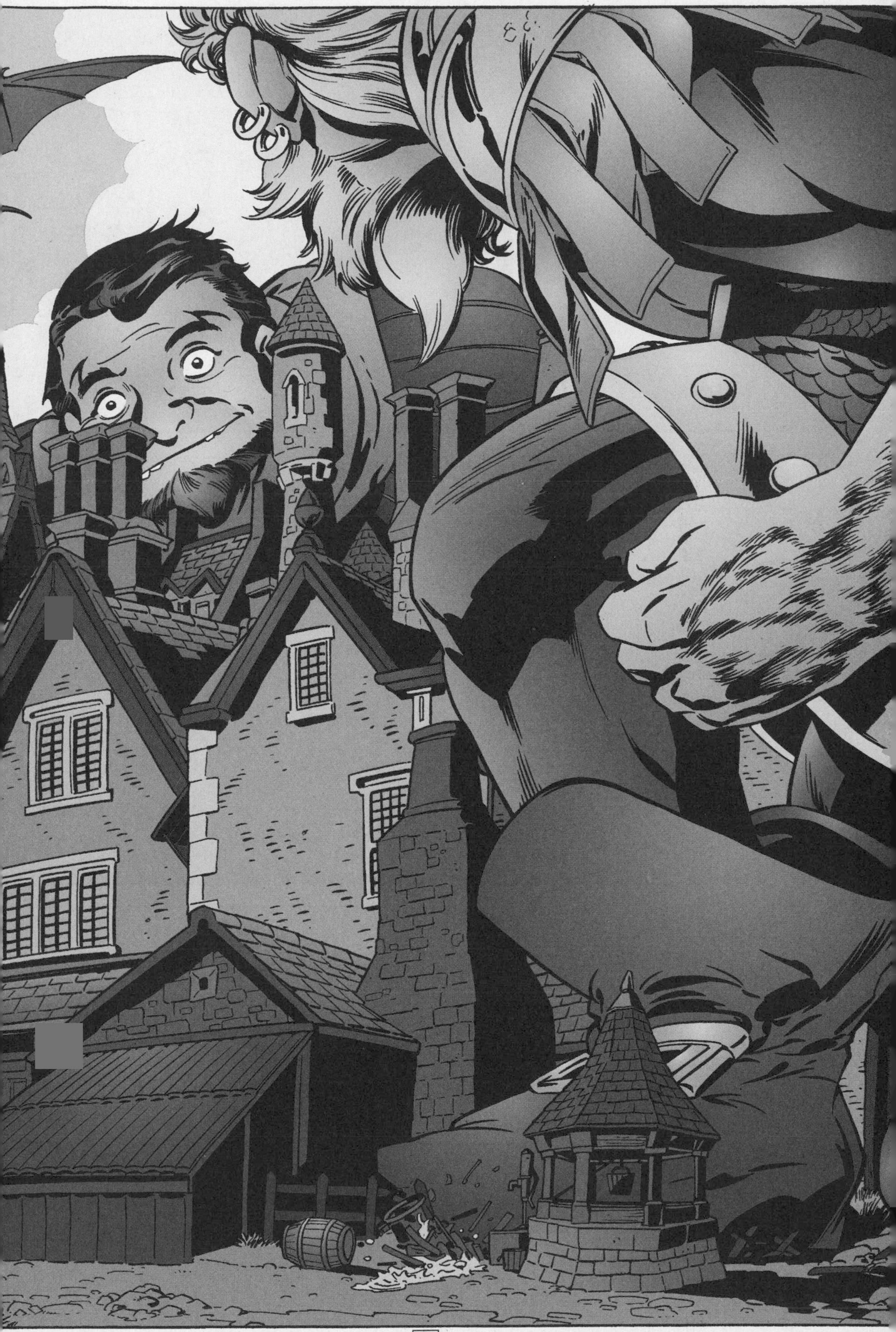

CAN'T YOU GO *FASTER?* MISS WHITE AND MISS RED COULD BE IN *TERRIBLE* TROUBLE!

WE SHOULD *NEVER* HAVE STOPPED BACK THERE!

EXCEPT THAT WE *HAD* TO, TO GET *DIRECTIONS,* AFTER *YOU* GOT US LOST, BLUE BOY.

IT'S NOT *MY* FAULT. I'M A *CITY* DWELLER. WHO CAN FOLLOW ALL THESE REMOTE COUNTRY ROADS?

SIT BACK AND MIND YOUR *MONKEY.* YOU'RE MAKING ME *NERVOUS.*

AND HE BETTER *NOT* BE SHITTING ALL OVER MY *NEW* LEATHER UPHOLSTERY.

LOOK! SOMETHING'S ON *FIRE!*

PRIVATE ROAD

AND THE GODDAMN THREE BROTHERS ARE *AWAKE!*

WHAT'S GOING *ON?*

OH LOOK, THE *CAVALRY* FINALLY ARRIVES.

WHAT *HAPPENED* UP HERE? ARE YOU ALL RIGHT?

WE....UH... WE CAME TO *RESCUE* YOU.

RELAX, BOYS. WE HAD SOME TROUBLE, BUT IT'S OVER NOW.

MY SISTER AND THE REST OF THESE FOOLS ARE UNDER ARREST.

YEAH, IT SEEMS I WAS A BAD GIRL AGAIN.

BE CAREFUL, THOUGH. ONE OF THE *RINGLEADERS* OF THIS FIASCO SLIPPED AWAY IN THE CONFUSION.

GOLDILOCKS.

SHE *MAY* STILL BE AROUND HERE SOMEWHERE.

AND SHE WAS *ARMED* THE LAST TIME I SAW HER.

INTRUSIVE BITCH.

POW!

SNOW!

NEXT: SNOWFALL!

Twilight of the Dogs — Part Five of Animal Farm

| Written & created by Bill Willingham | Pencilled by Mark Buckingham | Inked by Steve Leialoha | Lettered by Todd Klein | Colored and Separated by Daniel Vozzo | Cover art by James Jean | Assistant Ed. Mariah Huehner | Editor Shelly Bond |

...HNNGN?...

WELCOME BACK, SNOW.

...HNNWW RRNG?...

HOW LONG **WHAT?** DO YOU MEAN HOW LONG SINCE YOU WERE SHOT?

YOU'VE BEEN IN A COMA FOR JUST OVER SIX WEEKS. WE'VE ALL BEEN TAKING TURNS LOOKING AFTER YOU. KING COLE JUST HANDED YOU OFF TO ME THIS MORNING.

...WHHT HHUNN?...

I DON'T THINK YOU SHOULD TRY TO TALK JUST NOW. IF YOU PROMISE TO STAY CALM AND QUIET, I'LL BE HAPPY TO FILL YOU IN ON WHAT'S HAPPENED.

BUT ONLY FOR A MINUTE OR TWO.

THEN I NEED TO TELL DOCTOR SWINE-HEART THAT YOU'RE BACK AMONG US.

"UNDERSTAND THOUGH THAT I GET *MOST* OF THIS SECONDHAND, SINCE I'M STILL NOT ALLOWED UP AT THE FARM."

MOVE *BACK,* DAMN YOU ALL!

"THE FOILED REVOLUTION THREATENED TO FLARE UP AGAIN, IN THE CHAOS THAT IMMEDIATELY FOLLOWED YOUR SHOOTING.

♪♪♪ da-TA! da-TA! da-TA!

SETTLE DOWN, EVERY GOD-CURSED ONE OF YOU, OR I'LL GUN THE *LOT* OF YOU DOWN WHERE YOU STAND!

"BUT BOY BLUE, BLUEBEARD AND YOUR EX-HUSBAND QUICKLY TOOK CONTROL.

AND YOU, BOY, DON'T BLOW THAT BLOODY HORN AGAIN, OR I MIGHT *FORGET* YOU'RE ON OUR SIDE!

"I UNDERSTAND EVEN BOY BLUE'S *MONKEY* WAS OF SOME HELP, ALTHOUGH I CAN'T IMAGINE HOW. "

HEAVE TO, CHICKEN LITTLE! YOU CAN'T ESCAPE OUR SWIFT, SURE *JUSTICE!*

BUT I'M *INNOCENT!* I WAS *FRAMED!* MY HEART WAS *ALWAYS* WITH YOU GUYS! *HONEST!*

"ONCE A SEMBLANCE OF ORDER WAS RESTORED, THE LOYAL FABLES WERE FANNED OUT ON A SEARCH FOR GOLDILOCKS.

DO YOU REALLY THINK THERE'S A CHANCE SHE'S *STILL* NEARBY?

SHE'S HAD MORE THAN AN *HOUR* TO MAKE HER GETAWAY.

"THEY FOUND HER WEAPON WHERE SHE'D ABANDONED IT, BUT BY THEN SHE WAS LONG GONE.

SHE CAN'T HIDE FROM US FOREVER. WHERE CAN SHE *GO?*

CERTAINLY NOT BACK TO THE HOMELANDS. I HEAR THE ADVERSARY WANTS HER DEAD AT *LEAST* AS MUCH AS WE DO.

"AND LOSING GOLDILOCKS WAS THE *LEAST* OF THEIR PROBLEMS.

"THEY STILL HAD TO WORK OUT WHAT TO DO WITH THE TREASONOUS FABLES, AND WHAT TO DO WITH A WAKENED DRAGON AND THREE GIANTS."

I'M HUNGRY.

IT WAS HARD ENOUGH HIDING THEM FROM THE *MUNDYS* WHILE THEY WERE ASLEEP.

AND THAT'S ALL I'M GOING TO SAY FOR NOW, BECAUSE I REALLY NEED TO REPORT THAT YOU'VE FINALLY WOKEN UP.

AND I SUSPECT YOU NEED SOME *NON-COMA* REST.

KNIGHTS OF MALTA HOSPITAL

TWO MORE WEEKS PASS.

ONE GUEST AT A TIME, AND THAT'S *FINAL,* OR I'LL BAN *ALL* OF YOU.

IF YOU INSIST, DOCTOR.

KNIGHTS OF MALTA **HOSPITAL**

GOOD MORNING, BIGBY, IS IT YOUR TURN IN THE *BABY-SITTING* ROTATION AGAIN?

EVERY THIRD DAY, WHETHER YOU WANT ME OR *NOT.*

HOW DOES IT FEEL TO BE BACK ON *REAL* FOOD?

IF THIS BLAND MUSH *COUNTS* AS "REAL FOOD," THEN I'D JUST AS SOON THEY PUT THE *IV TUBES* BACK INTO ME.

I'LL SEE IF THEY CAN DO BETTER. OTHER THAN THE BAD *CUISINE,* HOW ARE YOU?

BORED OUT OF MY *MIND.* HELP ME BREAK OUT OF HERE AND I'M YOURS *FOREVER.*

SORRY, SNOWFALL, BUT I'M ON *THEIR* SIDE. YOU'RE STAYING PUT FOR NOW. YOU STILL HAVE A LONG WAY TO GO BEFORE YOU'RE OFFICIALLY "ALL BETTER."

THEN AT LEAST TELL ME THE LATEST NEWS, DAY AFTER DAY OF MUNDY TV IS ROTTING WHAT'S LEFT OF MY *BRAIN.*

WELL, THE *WAR TRIALS* HAVE STARTED.

STAY IN LINE! *NO* TALKING!

REMEMBER: IF YOU WISH TO PRESENT EVIDENCE IN MITIGATION, EXTENUATION OR EVEN REFUTATION OF *ANY* CHARGES, IT IS UP TO *YOU* TO MENTION IT WHEN YOU GET TO THE FRONT OF THE LINE.

NEXT?

KING LOUIE, OF THE KIPLING GROUP OF FABLES.

CHARGES?

ACTIVELY AIDING THE REVOLUTIONARIES, BUT NOT ONE OF THE RINGLEADERS. HE TOOK PART IN THE HUNT FOR SNOW WHITE.

DO YOU DISPUTE THESE CHARGES OR INSIST ON A FORMAL TRIAL?

NO, I GUESS NOT.

THEN I SENTENCE YOU TO TWENTY YEARS OF HARD LABOR, REDUCED TO FIVE YEARS, CONDITIONAL ON YOUR GOOD BEHAVIOR.

KING LOUIS...

BOP

NEXT.

REYNARD THE FOX. NO CHARGES. HE ACTIVELY RESISTED THE REVOLUTIONARIES AND THEREBY SAVED SNOW WHITE'S LIFE.

FOR WHICH THE FABLE COMMUNITY OWES YOU A DEBT OF *GRATITUDE.*

I HOPE YOU'LL FORGIVE US FOR PUTTING OFF ANY FORMAL RECOGNITION OF YOUR INSPIRATIONAL ACTS OF HEROISM FOR ANOTHER OCCASION.

NO PROBLEM. *GLAD* TO HELP.

NEXT.

POSEY PIG. REVOLUTIONARY RINGLEADER. COMPLICIT IN THE MURDER OF COLIN PIG, THE KIDNAPPING AND ENSLAVEMENT OF WEYLAND SMITH AND THE ATTEMPTED MURDER OF SNOW WHITE.

IN MY *OWN* DEFENSE, I'D LIKE TO SAY THAT--

SAVE IT FOR LATER.

POSEY PIG IS ORDERED HELD OVER FOR FORMAL TRIBUNAL IN CONTEMPLATION OF CAPITAL PUNISHMENT.

BOP

TAKE THE PIG INTO CUSTODY.

NEXT.

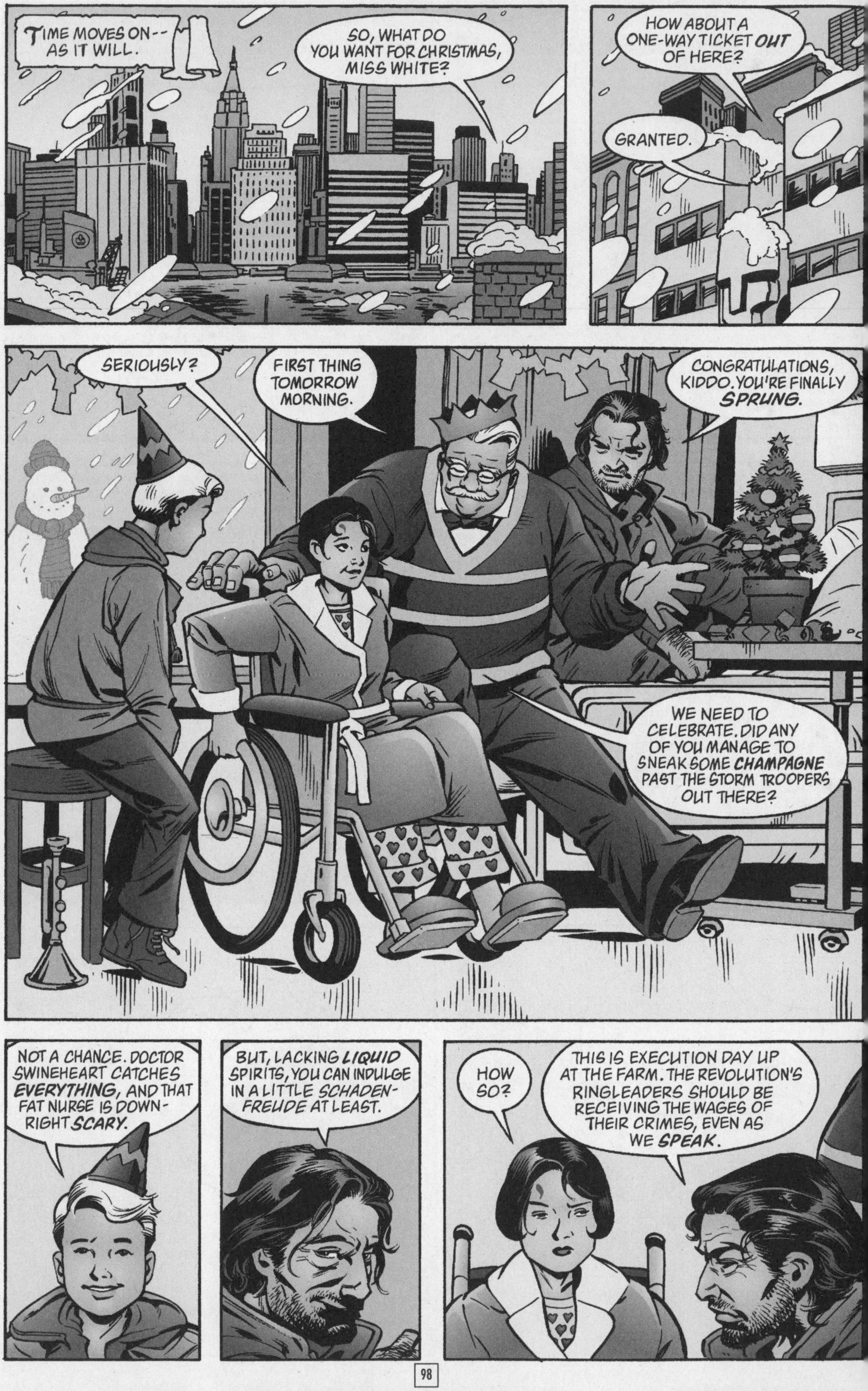
TIME MOVES ON-- AS IT WILL.
SO, WHAT DO YOU WANT FOR CHRISTMAS, MISS WHITE?
HOW ABOUT A ONE-WAY TICKET OUT OF HERE?
GRANTED.
SERIOUSLY?
FIRST THING TOMORROW MORNING.
CONGRATULATIONS, KIDDO. YOU'RE FINALLY SPRUNG.
WE NEED TO CELEBRATE. DID ANY OF YOU MANAGE TO SNEAK SOME CHAMPAGNE PAST THE STORM TROOPERS OUT THERE?
NOT A CHANCE. DOCTOR SWINEHEART CATCHES EVERYTHING, AND THAT FAT NURSE IS DOWN-RIGHT SCARY.
BUT, LACKING LIQUID SPIRITS, YOU CAN INDULGE IN A LITTLE SCHADEN-FREUDE AT LEAST.
HOW SO?
THIS IS EXECUTION DAY UP AT THE FARM. THE REVOLUTION'S RINGLEADERS SHOULD BE RECEIVING THE WAGES OF THEIR CRIMES, EVEN AS WE SPEAK.

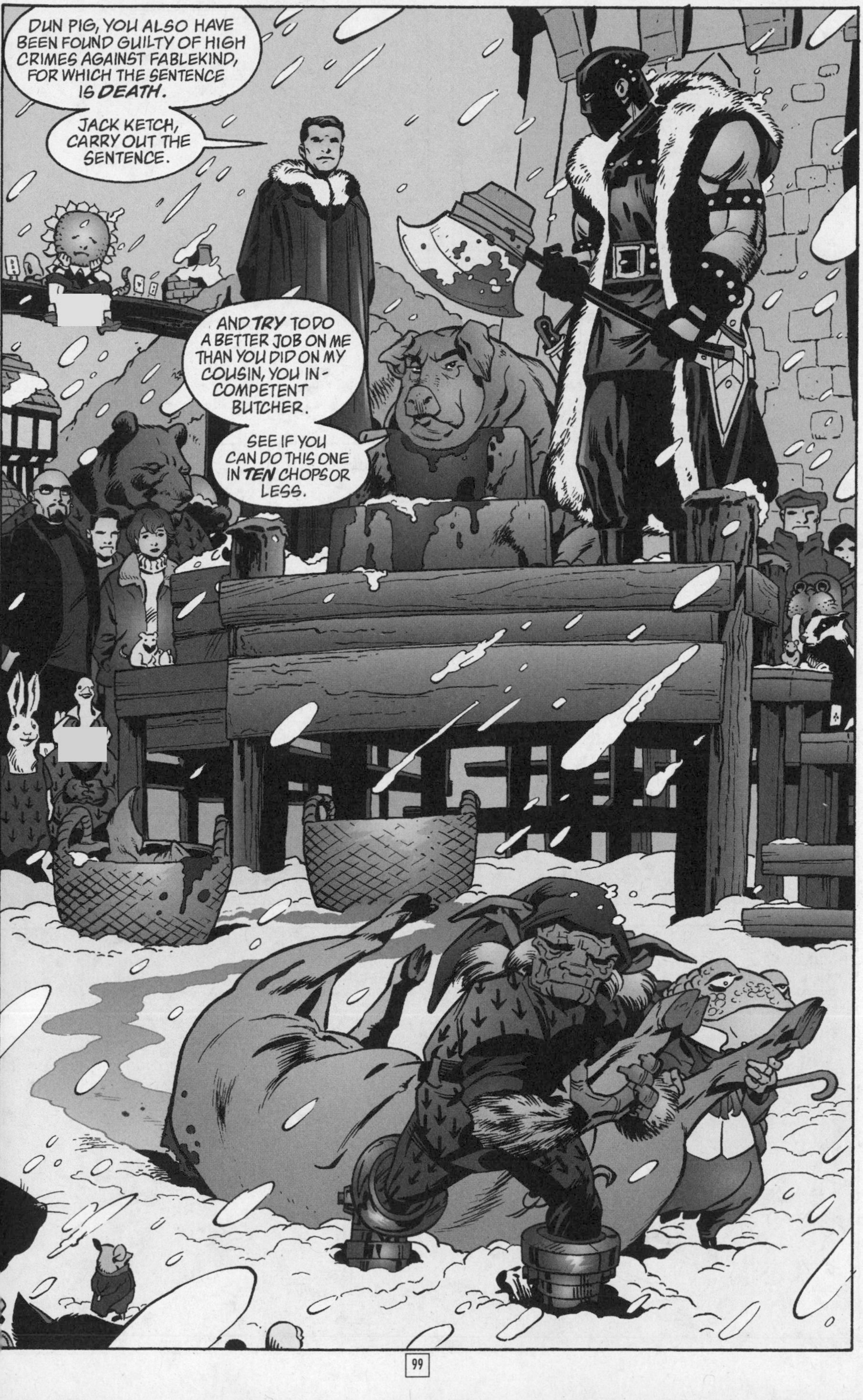
DUN PIG, YOU ALSO HAVE BEEN FOUND GUILTY OF HIGH CRIMES AGAINST FABLEKIND, FOR WHICH THE SENTENCE IS DEATH.
JACK KETCH, CARRY OUT THE SENTENCE.
AND TRY TO DO A BETTER JOB ON ME THAN YOU DID ON MY COUSIN, YOU IN-COMPETENT BUTCHER.
SEE IF YOU CAN DO THIS ONE IN TEN CHOPS OR LESS.

THE FOLLOWING MORNING...

HOW DID THE FARM FABLES TAKE IT?

ABOUT AS WELL AS COULD BE EXPECTED, CONSIDERING THE BAD DAYS THAT *PRECEDED* IT AND MADE IT NECESSARY.

IT'LL TAKE SOME TIME BEFORE THINGS GET BACK TO NORMAL UP THERE.

IF THINGS *EVER* DO.

IT'LL HAPPEN, SNOW. ONE OF THE ADVANTAGES OF *NEAR* IMMORTALITY IS THAT WE CAN LEARN TO ACCEPT AND ADAPT TO MOST ANYTHING-- EVENTUALLY.

I SUPPOSE SO, WHICH BRINGS US, MORE OR LESS, TO THE *ONE* SUBJECT THAT YOU'VE EACH MADE SURE TO AVOID AROUND ME.

AND THAT WOULD BE *WHAT?*

I KNOW YOU'VE BEEN *PROTECTING* ME UNTIL I WAS WELL ENOUGH, AND I APPRECIATE IT, BIGBY, BUT NOW IT'S TIME TO TELL ME ABOUT ROSE RED.

WHEN DOES MY *SISTER* GO UP ON THE *CHOPPING BLOCK?* OR HAS IT ALREADY *HAPPENED?*

WHAT THE *HELL* ARE YOU TALKING ABOUT?

WELCOME BACK, SNOW.

HOW ARE YOU FEELING?

WHEN WILL YOU BE BACK TO WORK?

SHE WAS ONE OF THE *RINGLEADERS.* EVEN THOUGH SHE JOINED LATE, SHE--

ARE YOU *JOKING?*

I NEED TO RENEGOTIATE MY RENT AGAIN...

DO YOU *SERIOUSLY* NOT KNOW WHAT HAPPENED UP THERE? WHAT SHE *DID?*

I THOUGHT SO. SHE MADE IT PRETTY *CLEAR* TO ME AT THE TIME. WHAT DO YOU THINK NEEDS FURTHER EXPLANATION?

WELCOME *HOME*, MISS WHITE. WE MISSED YOU *DEARLY* THESE PAST MONTHS.

ARE YOU COMPLETELY *UNAWARE* THAT SHE SAVED YOUR LIFE?

EXCUSE ME?

IT ALL CAME OUT AT HER HEARING.

THE REVOLUTIONARIES HAD JUST KILLED COLIN AND AFTER CUTTING YOU *ENTIRELY* OFF FROM OUTSIDE CONTACT, IT WAS OBVIOUS TO *HER* --IF NOT *YOU*--THAT THE TWO OF YOU WERE NEXT.

IT WAS UNLIKELY YOU'D SURVIVE THE *NIGHT*, IN FACT.

SO ROSE *CONVINCED* THE REVOLUTIONARIES THAT HER SYMPATHIES WERE WITH THEM. SHE WAS *RELUCTANTLY* PERSUADED TO JOIN THEM, BUT ONLY ON THE CONDITION THAT THEY DIDN'T OUTRIGHT *MURDER* YOU.

YEAH, OKAY, SHE SAID *SOMETHING* LIKE THAT, AT ONE POINT, BUT I THOUGHT--

SHE BOUGHT *ENOUGH* TIME FOR ONE OF YOU TO FIGURE A WAY OUT OF YOUR PREDICAMENT--WHICH *YOU* EVENTUALLY DID.

GOD STRIKE ME DOWN FOR A *FOOL*, BIGBY. I NEVER *REALIZED*--

WELL, AS I LIVE AND **BREATHE**, IF IT ISN'T THE VERY WEYLAND SMITH, ESQUIRE, COME DOWN FROM THE FARM ON THE FIRST WARM DAY OF THE SPRING. **TWO** UNEXPECTED PLEASURES AT ONCE.

HELLO, JOHN. IT'S NOT UNEXPECTED FOR **EVERYONE**, I'M SORRY TO SAY.

SNOW WHITE'S SUMMONED ME DOWN HERE, MOST LIKELY TO **SACK** ME, FOR THE WAY I SCREWED UP MY ADMINISTRATION OF THE FARM.

OH DEAR. SOME DARK **BUSINESS** THAT WAS LAST YEAR. **TERRIBLE** DAYS.

TELL ME ABOUT IT.

I DON'T **BLAME** YOU FOR WHAT HAPPENED UP THERE, WEYLAND.

BUSINESS OFFICE
S. WHITE

WE HAVEN'T **YET** BEEN CORRUPTED BY THE MUNDYS' MODERN SOCIAL PHILOSOPHY CONCERNING SUCH THINGS. THE RESPONSIBILITY LIES ENTIRELY WITH THE **PERPETRATORS**, AND NOT THEIR VICTIMS.

I'M RELIEVED TO HEAR THAT, SNOW.

JUST THE SAME, THOUGH, YOU HAVE TO REALIZE THERE'S NO WAY YOU CAN RESUME ADMINISTRATION OF THE FARM.

YES. I KNEW, ONE WAY OR ANOTHER, I WAS FINISHED THERE THE NIGHT THEY FIRST CAME FOR ME. YOU NEED A BOSS WHO CAN CONTINUE TO COMMAND THEIR RESPECT.

I'M SORRY, WEYLAND.

NOT AT ALL. TO TELL YOU THE TRUTH, I'M ACTUALLY LOOKING FORWARD TO MOVING DOWN TO THE CITY FOR THE FIRST TIME IN-- WHAT? HAS IT BEEN A FULL **CENTURY** NOW?

I'LL APPROVE IT, IF THAT'S YOUR *DECISION*, BUT I WONDER IF I CAN TALK YOU INTO TAKING ON A *NEW* TASK FIRST.

YES?

LET'S STROLL A BIT. SOMEWHERE WE CAN TALK MORE *PRIVATELY*.

YOU PUSH.

THOSE CAVES UPSTATE ARE STILL FULL OF MUNDY *FIREARMS*, RIGHT? WOULD YOU CONSIDER CONTINUING TO ADAPT THEM FOR USE BY NON-HUMAN FABLES?

HUH? BUT I THOUGHT YOU *DIDN'T* SUPPORT--

NO, I SUPPORTED NEITHER THEIR REVOLUTION *NOR* THEIR METHODS. BUT THEIR IDEA TO CREATE *MODERN ARMS* WE CAN USE AGAINST THE ADVERSARY IS A GOOD ONE.

WE'D BE *FOOLS* NOT TO FOLLOW UP ON IT.

YOU WANT TO *INVADE* THE HOMELANDS?

OF COURSE. NOT TODAY, NOT THIS YEAR, AND PROBABLY NOT EVEN THIS *DECADE*--BUT SOMEDAY, YES.

THE ADVERSARY HAS US VASTLY OUTNUMBERED IN RAW TROOP STRENGTH. AND HE HAS A *HUNDRED* WITCHES OR SORCERERS TO EVERY *ONE* OF OURS. WE NEED AN *ADVANTAGE* IN WEAPONS SYSTEMS.

SO, WILL YOU CONTINUE PROVIDING IT TO US? ONLY NOT *CHAINED UP* THIS TIME, OF COURSE. YOU'D BE FREE TO WORK AT WHATEVER PACE SUITS YOU.

I'LL CONSIDER IT.

THANK YOU. LET'S GO THIS WAY.

IF YOU'LL PUT ME UP IN ONE OF THE WOODLAND'S GUEST ROOMS TONIGHT, WE CAN CONTINUE THIS TOMORROW.

IN THE MEANTIME, I'VE GOT A BIT OF A *SURPRISE* FOR YOU, THOUGH I HAVE NO CERTAINTY IF IT'S A GOOD ONE--OR OTHERWISE.

YES? WHAT IS IT?

ROSE RED RODE DOWN FROM THE FARM WITH ME. SHE'S BEEN DOING GREAT WORK UP THERE, BUT I THINK SHE'S FINALLY READY TO SEE YOU FACE-TO-FACE.

SHE'S WAITING OUT IN THE TRUCK, IN CASE YOU'RE NOT UP TO SEEING HER YET.

GO ON IN. SHE'S WAITING FOR YOU IN THE CHAPEL. THAT SMALL ONE BACK IN --

I KNOW THE WAY.

SO, HERE I AM. THE PRODIGAL *RETURNS*, AND ALL THAT.

COME IN. UHM, I..., UH...

OBVIOUSLY JUST IN TIME FOR THE LATEST IN A NEVER-ENDING STRING OF AWKWARD *MOMENTS* BETWEEN ESTRANGED SISTERS.

I HOPE NOT. AT LEAST I *HOPE* WE CAN WORK THROUGH IT SOMEDAY, AND MAYBE GET BACK TO THE WAY WE WERE SO LONG AGO.

DO YOU REALLY THINK THAT'S LIKELY? OR EVEN *POSSIBLE*?

YES, I DO. BECAUSE I FORGAVE YOU LONG AGO FOR WHAT YOU DID.

OH? HOW PERFECTLY *NOBLE* OF YOU.

BUT WHAT IF I HAVEN'T FORGIVEN *YOU* YET?

FOR *WHAT?* WHAT DID I EVER DO TO *YOU* TO DESERVE SO MANY YEARS OF OPEN *SCORN?*

ISN'T IT *OBVIOUS,* EVEN TO ONE AS *OBLIVIOUS* AS YOU?

I GUESS YOU'LL HAVE TO *SPELL IT OUT* FOR ME.

LOOK AT YOU! YOU'RE *ALIVE!*

I WAS STANDING RIGHT NEXT TO YOU AS HALF OF YOUR *HEAD* WAS BLOWN ALL OVER MY *FUCKING* SHIRT!

YOUR SKULL AND *BRAINS* WERE ALL-- AND YET YOU GOT *BETTER!* HOW IS THAT EVEN *POSSIBLE?*

I DON'T KNOW.

UNFORTUNATELY I *DO.* THE MUNDYS *ADORE* YOU BY THE *MILLIONS,* BY THE *HUNDREDS* OF MILLIONS!

THEY KEEP MAKING THEIR GODAWFUL ANIMATED MOVIES AND WRITING THEIR ENDLESS CHILDREN'S STORIES ABOUT *YOU.* SO YOU *CAN'T* DIE!

THEY'LL NEVER *LET* YOU!

BUT WHO REMEMBERS *ME?* NOT ONE IN A MILLION OF THEM! IT USED TO BE SNOW WHITE *AND* ROSE RED. NOW IT'S JUST SNOW WHITE, *PERIOD.* ALL ALONE! NO SISTER NEEDED OR *DESIRED*, THANK YOU SO VERY MUCH!

IF IT HAD BEEN *ME* WHO'D TAKEN THAT BULLET, I'D BE DEAD AS A *DOORNAIL.*

AND HOW IS THAT *MY* FAULT?

"WHEN WE WERE YOUNG, BACK IN THE CABIN, WE *PLEDGED* WE'D BE TO-GETHER *FOREVER.*

"YOU AND ME AGAINST THE WORLD... *REMEMBER?*"

BUT THE *MOMENT* YOUR PRETTY PRINCE CHARMING CAME ALONG, YOU RODE OFF WITH HIM, WITHOUT SO MUCH AS A BACKWARD *GLANCE.*

IT WASN'T *LIKE* THAT. I SENT FOR YOU TO COME LIVE WITH US.

EVENTUALLY.

AND THAT WAS MY GREAT *CRIME?* IT TOOK ME TOO *LONG* TO SEND FOR YOU? THAT'S WHY YOU SEDUCED HIM, AND RUINED MY MARRIAGE -- ALL TO *PUNISH* ME?

BINGO.

FINE. THEN YOU *HAD* YOUR REVENGE LONG AGO. WHY ARE THE CLAWS STILL OUT AFTER ALL THESE YEARS?

BECAUSE YOU'RE STILL THE *POPULAR* ONE AND I'M FED UP WITH LIVING IN YOUR SHADOW.

THEN *DO* SOMETHING ABOUT IT.

I ALREADY HAVE. I'VE BEEN WORKING UP AT THE FARM, FIRST TO WORK OFF MY PUBLIC SERVICE DEBT--

THAT WAS FINISHED AT LEAST SIX MONTHS AGO.

--AND THEN BECAUSE IT KEPT ME AWAY FROM *YOU*. SURPRISE--*FIRST* I FOUND OUT I WAS GOOD AT IT AND *THEN* FOUND OUT I LIKED IT.

SO ALL THAT'S LEFT IS TO *FORMALIZE* THE ARRANGEMENT. YOU NEED A NEW FARM ADMINISTRATOR.

YOU?

WHY *NOT* ME? WEYLAND IS OUT, AND I CAN DO THE JOB. YOU RUN THE CITY FABLETOWN AND I RUN THE FARM, SO AT LONG LAST WE'RE BACK TO BEING *EQUALS* AGAIN.

I CAN HANDLE THAT. CAN *YOU*?

"AS MY FIRST OFFICIAL DUTY, I'VE ALREADY COME UP WITH A SOLUTION TO OUR GIANTS AND DRAGON PROBLEM. THEY DON'T WANT TO GO BACK TO SLEEP FOR HUNDREDS OF YEARS AND WHO CAN *BLAME* THEM? BUT IN THEIR PRESENT FORM WE COULD NEVER KEEP THEM OUT OF SIGHT, AND JUST KEEPING THEM *FED* IS ALREADY THREATENING TO STRIP THE FARM BARE. SO WHAT WE HAVE TO DO IS MAKE A SACRIFICE IN THE *SHORT* TERM TO PREVENT A DISASTER IN THE *LONG* RUN."

OKAY, LISTEN *UP*, KIDS, BECAUSE THIS IS WHAT WE'RE GOING TO DO.

DO YOU GUYS KNOW WHAT A "PERMANENT TRANSFORMATION" SPELL IS?

"ALL YOU HAVE TO DO IS AUTHORIZE THE USE OF THE DISCRETIONARY SPENDING BUDGET FOR *BOTH* FABLETOWNS FOR THE REST OF THIS YEAR, AND PROBABLY THE NEXT. WE HAVE TO BUY A *VERY* EXPENSIVE SET OF ENCHANTMENTS."

AND SOON ENOUGH...

LADIES AND GENTLEMEN-- IMPORTANT VISITING *INDIGNITARIES*-- SINCE THE ORIGINALS ARE *DEAD*, MEET THE "THREE LITTLE PIGS" PART *TWO*.

JOHNNY, DONNY AND LONNY: FORMERLY GIANTS OF RENOWN.

SO WHERE'S OUR NEW COTTAGE?

WONDERFUL.

YOU DID IT.

WELL DONE, ROSE.

THE MUNDYS' NEED FOR THREE LITTLE PIGS TO MATCH THEIR BELOVED STORY IS SATISFIED. AND NOT A ONE OF THEM WOULD KNOW OR CARE THAT THEY'RE DIFFERENT PIGGIES, WITH DIFFERENT NAMES.

WHAT ABOUT CLARATHEA, THE DRAGON?

CLARA IS NOW MY NEW *BEST FRIEND* AND ENFORCER.

ENFORCER? HOW?

SHOW THEM, SWEETIE.

WE DECIDED TO HOLD ONTO ONE OF HER MORE *ADVANTAGEOUS* DRAGON QUALITIES. NO MORE REVOLUTIONS HERE.

WHOOOSH!

CHARMING.

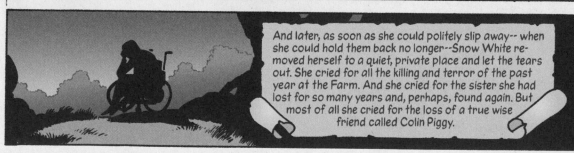

And later, as soon as she could politely slip away-- when she could hold them back no longer--Snow White removed herself to a quiet, private place and let the tears out. She cried for all the killing and terror of the past year at the Farm. And she cried for the sister she had lost for so many years and, perhaps, found again. But most of all she cried for the loss of a true wise friend called Colin Piggy.

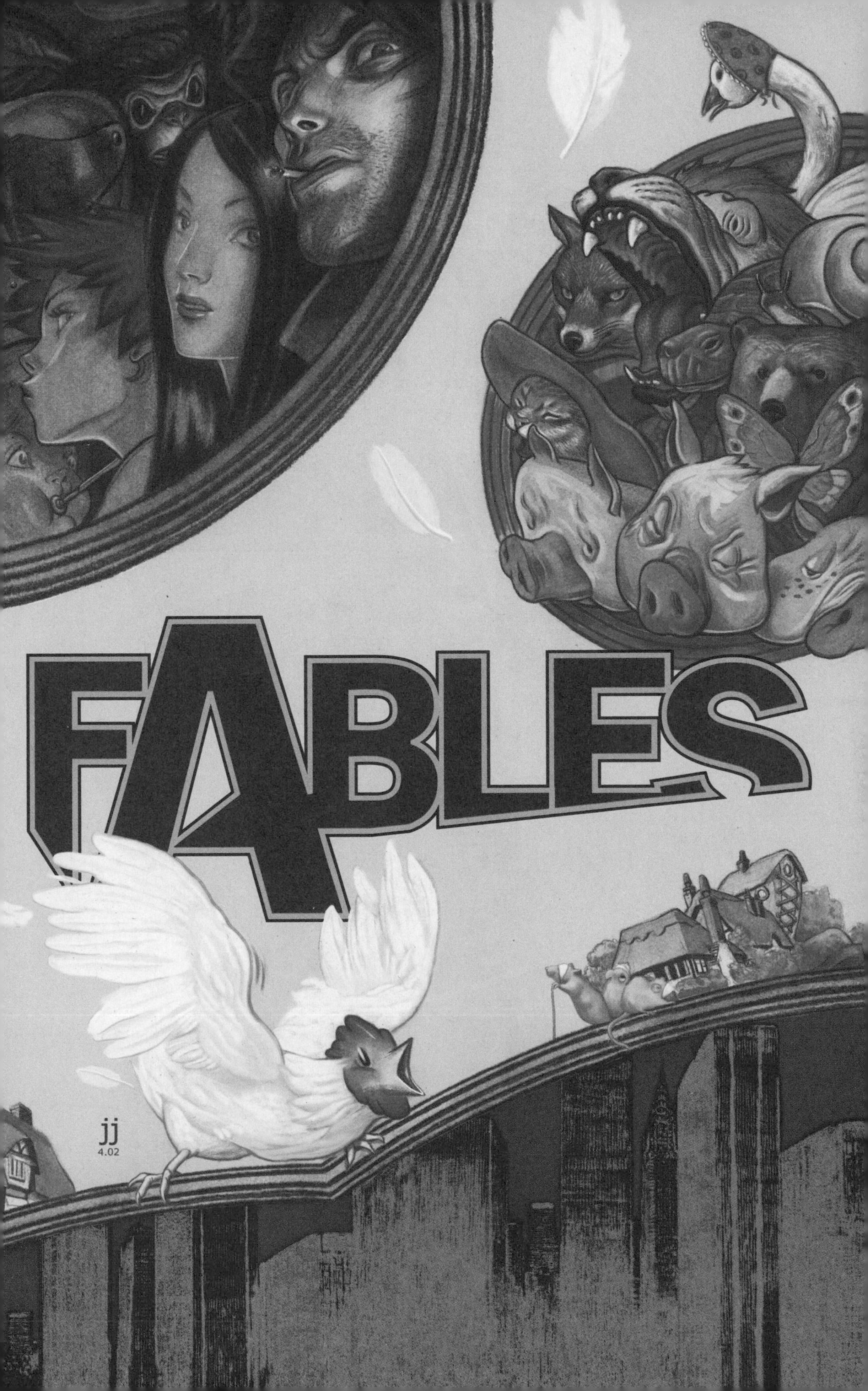
FABLES
jj
4.02

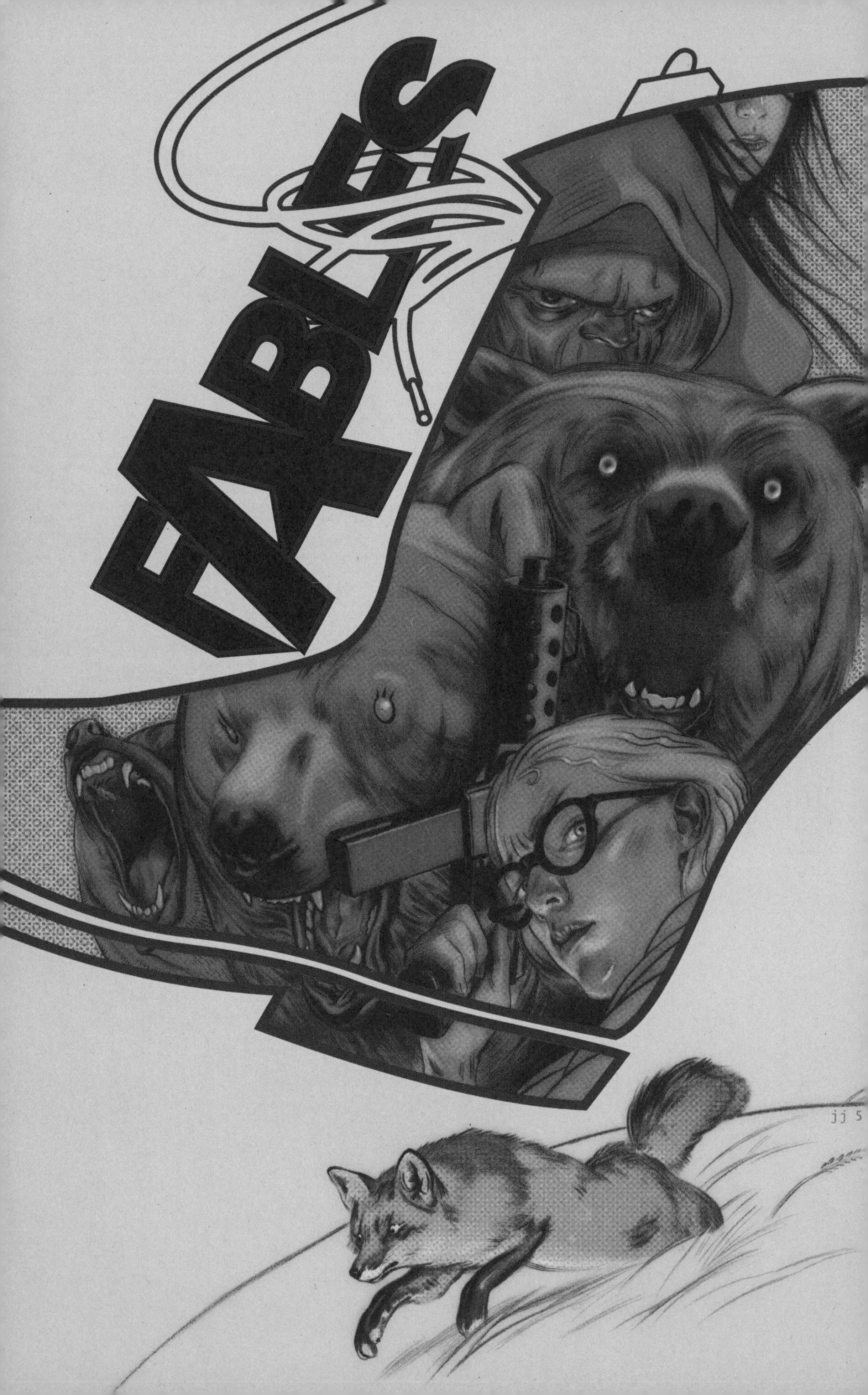
FABLES

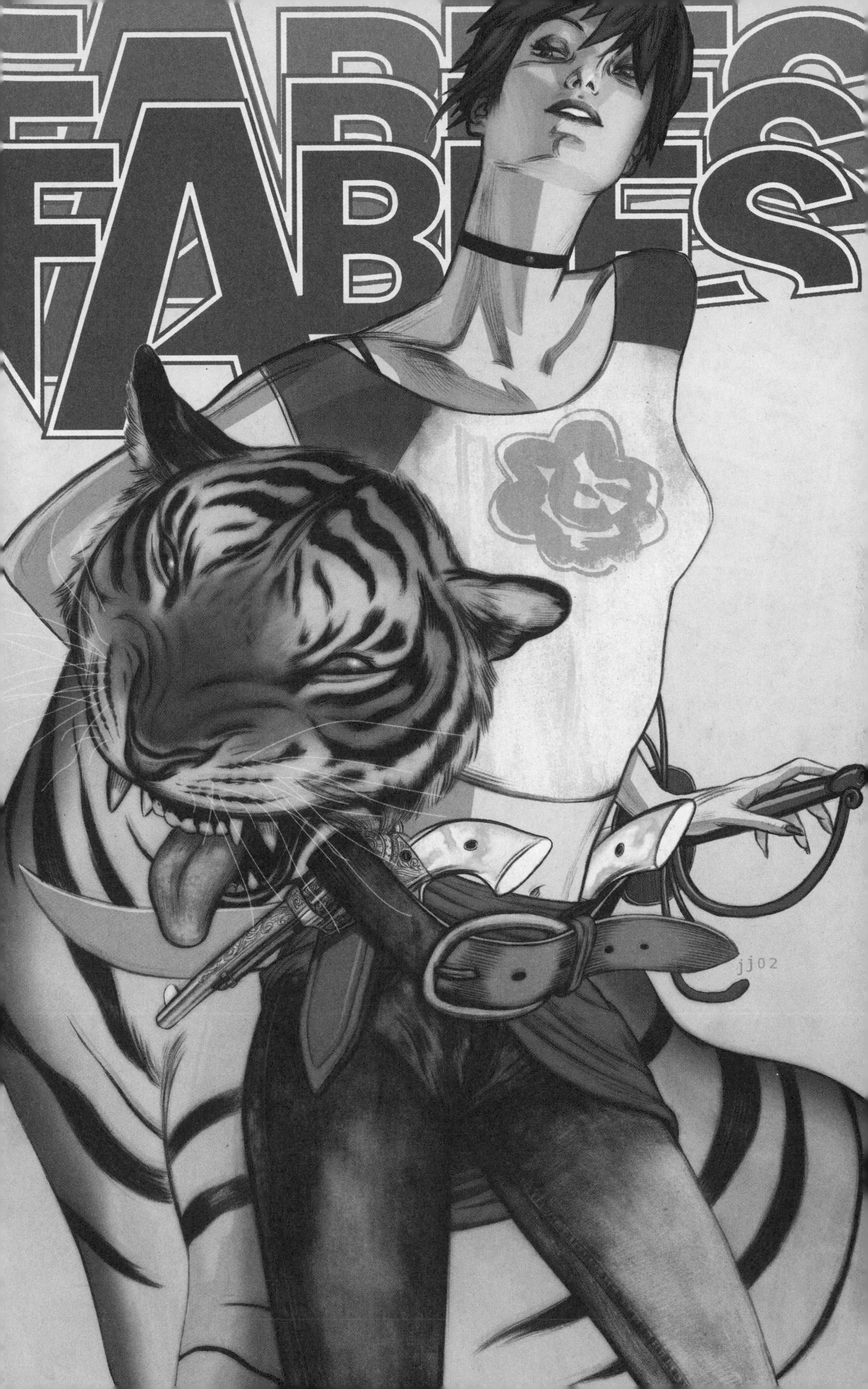
FABLES
jj02

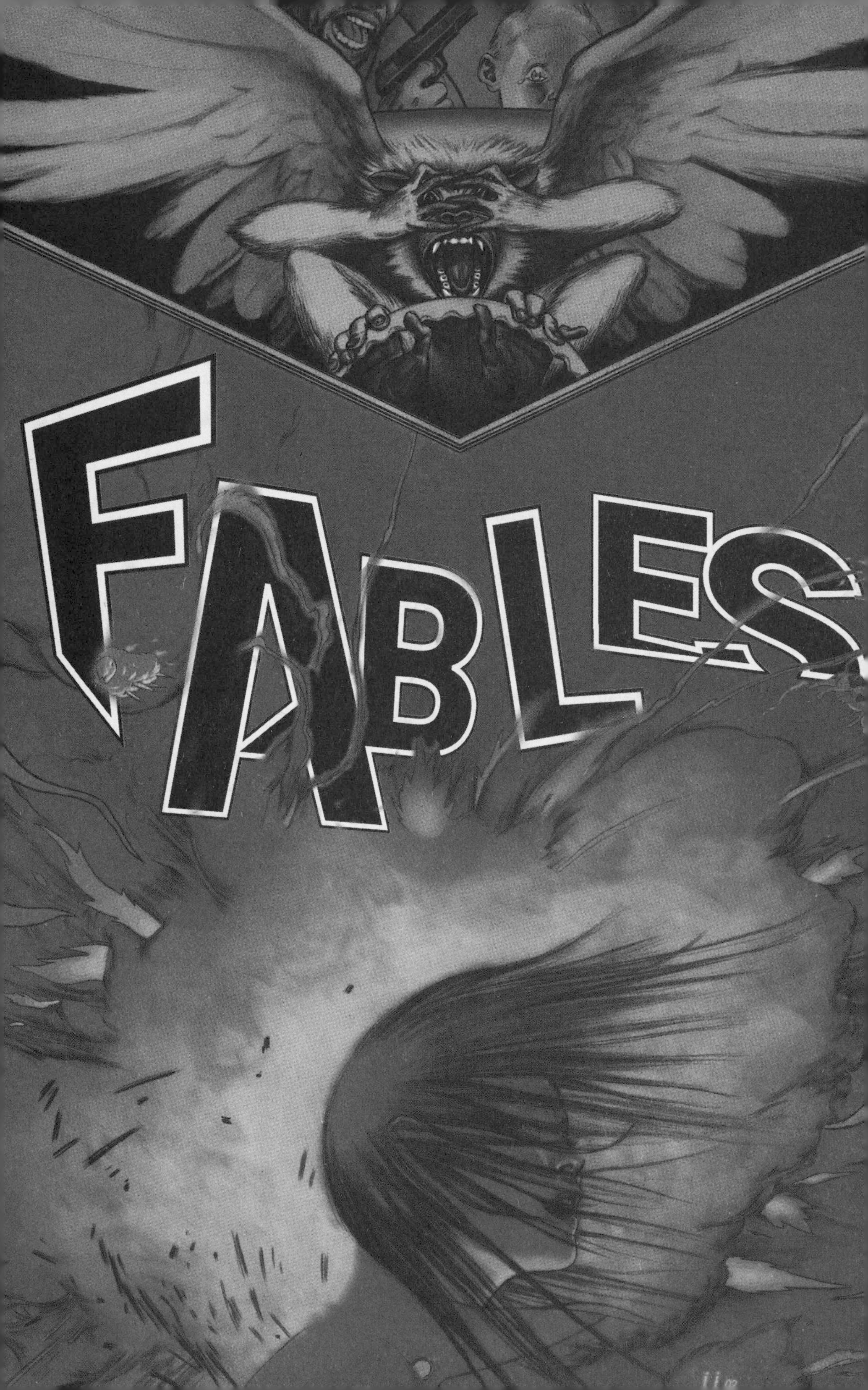
FABLES

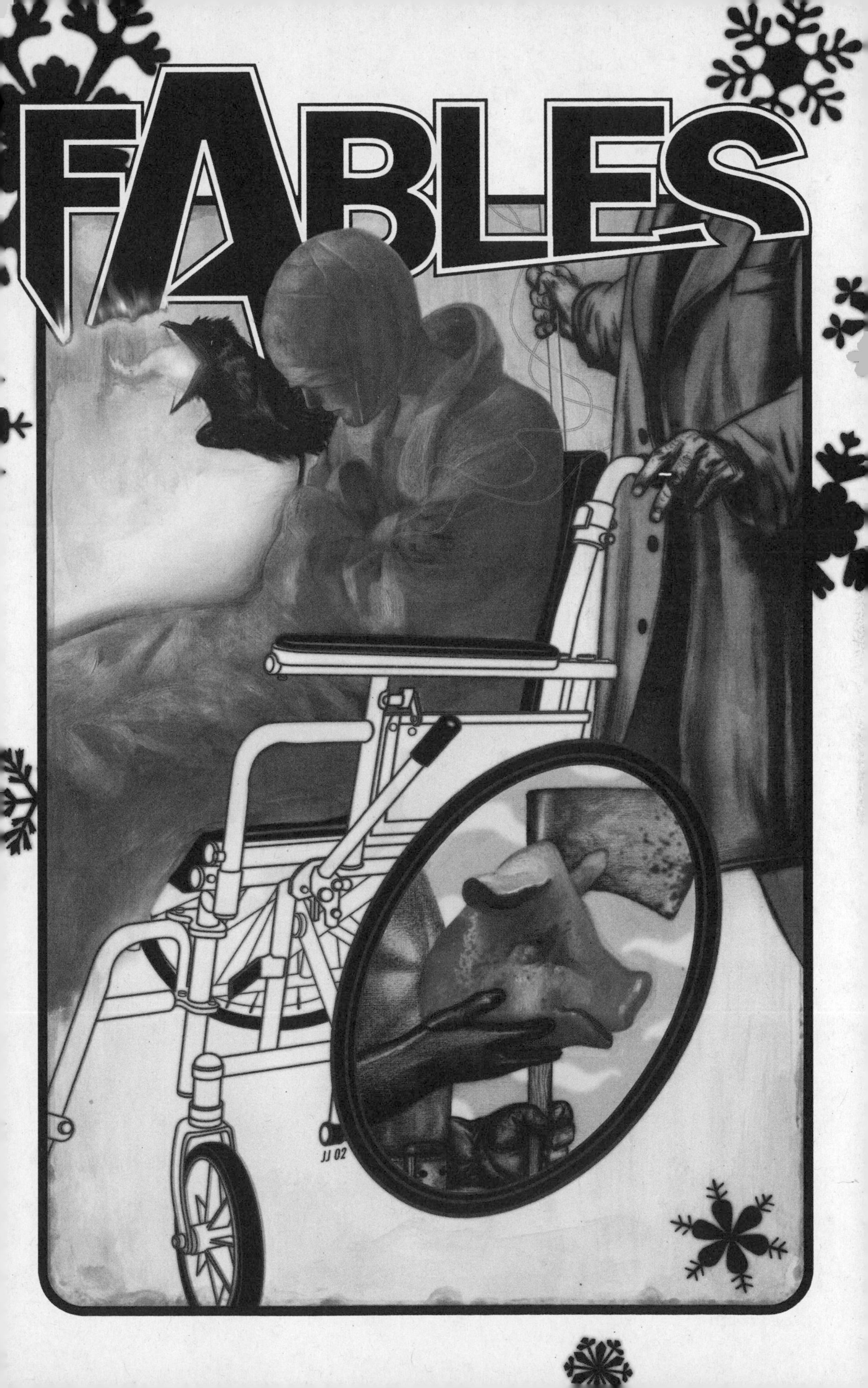
FABLES
JJ 02

Cover sketch for FABLES #6

⚓ ONCE UPON A TIME... ⚓

A selection of cover pencils, character sketches, and original character designs

from James Jean, Mark Buckingham, and Bill Willingham.

PRELIMINARY COVER PENCILS BY JAMES JEAN

Cover sketch for FABLES: ANIMAL FARM

Early cover sketch for FABLES #7

Cover sketch for FABLES #9

Early cover sketch for FABLES #8

Cover sketch for FABLES #10

CHARACTER SKETCHES BY MARK BUCKINGHAM

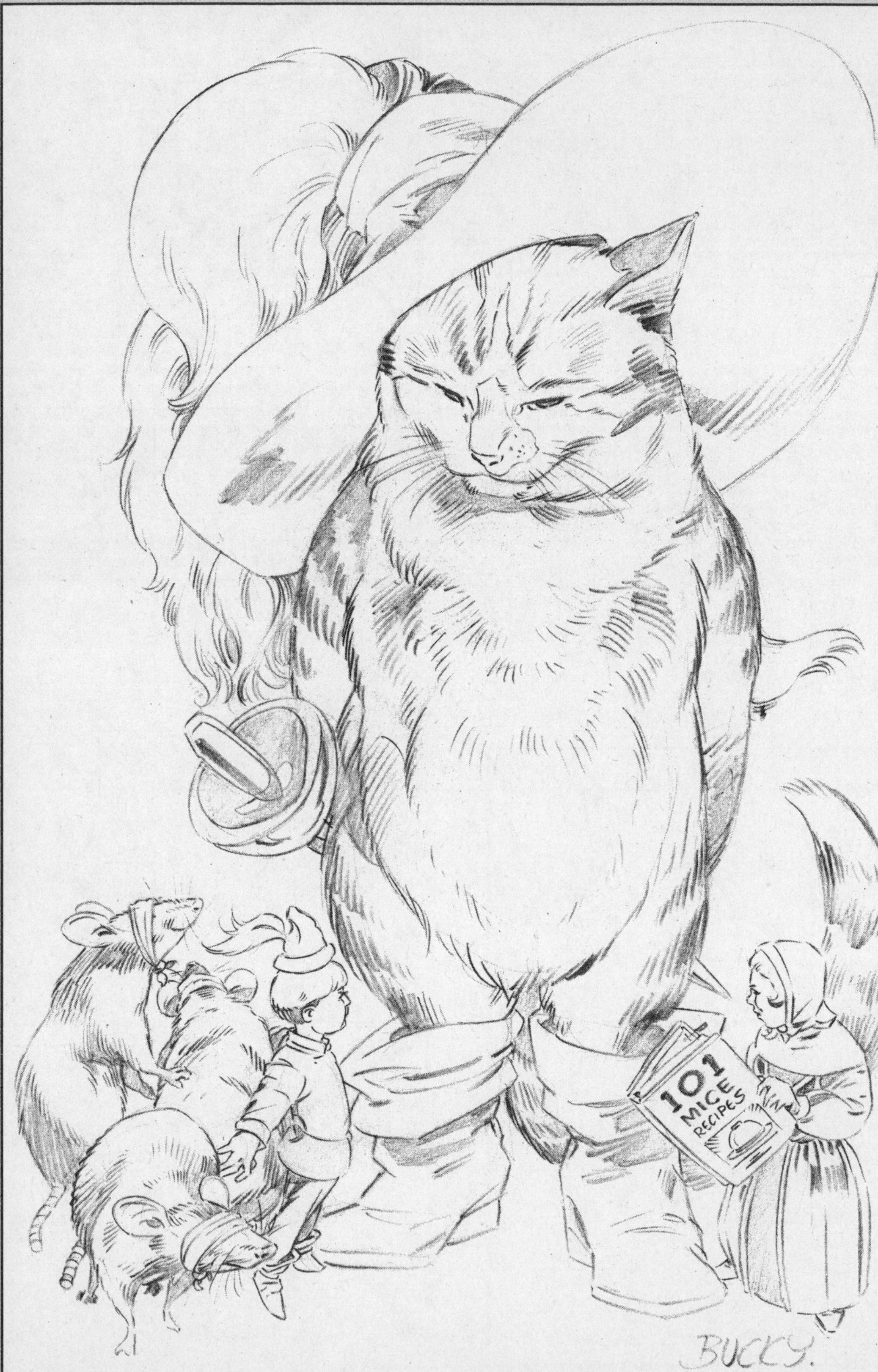
101
MICE
RECIPES
BUCKY.

DUN.

POSEY.

THE THREE PIG'S.

COLIN.

BUCKY.

ORIGINAL CHARACTER DESIGNS BY BILL WILLINGHAM

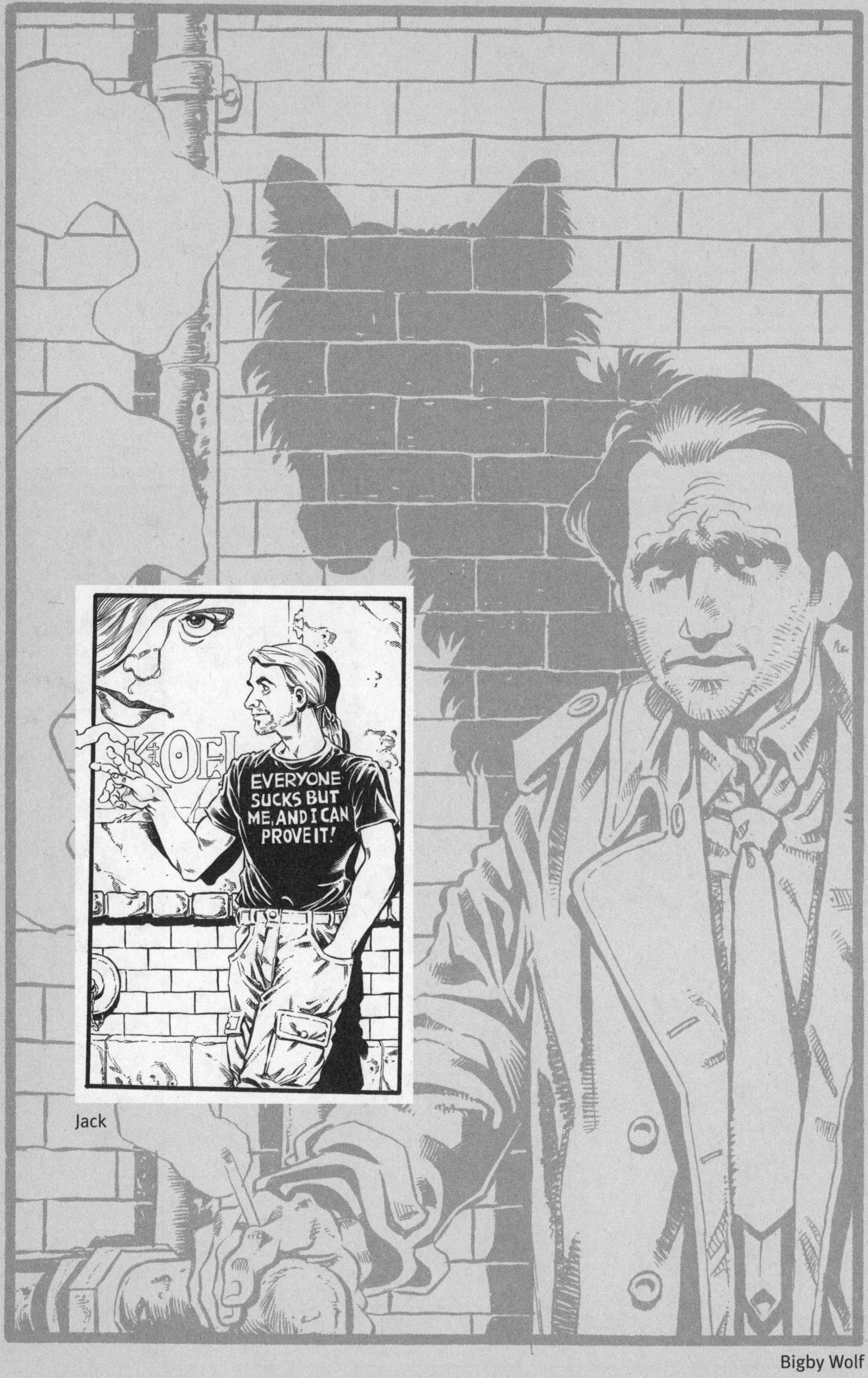
EVERYONE SUCKS BUT ME, AND I CAN PROVE IT!

Jack

Bigby Wolf

Snow White and
Little Boy Blue

Prince Charming

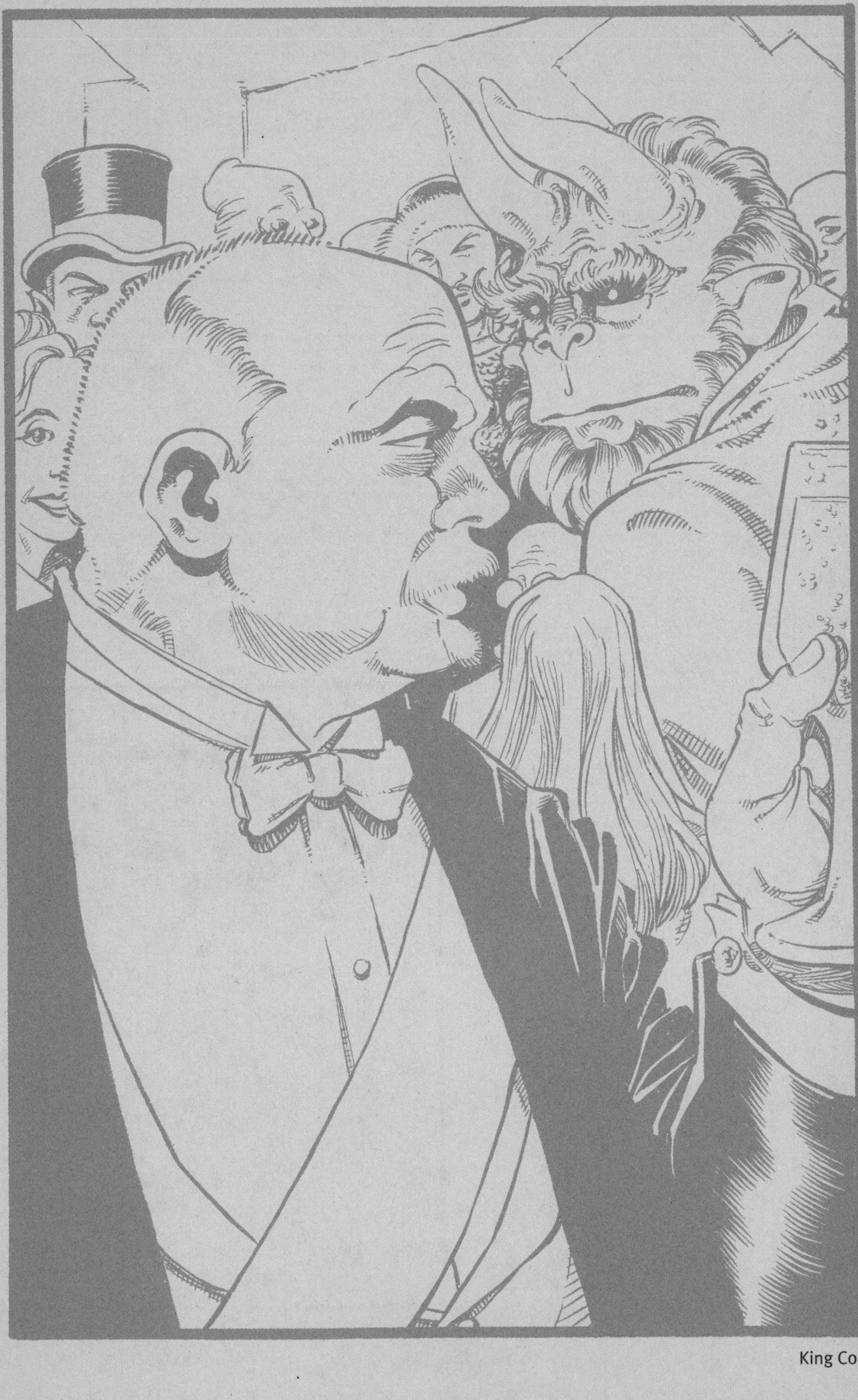

King Cole

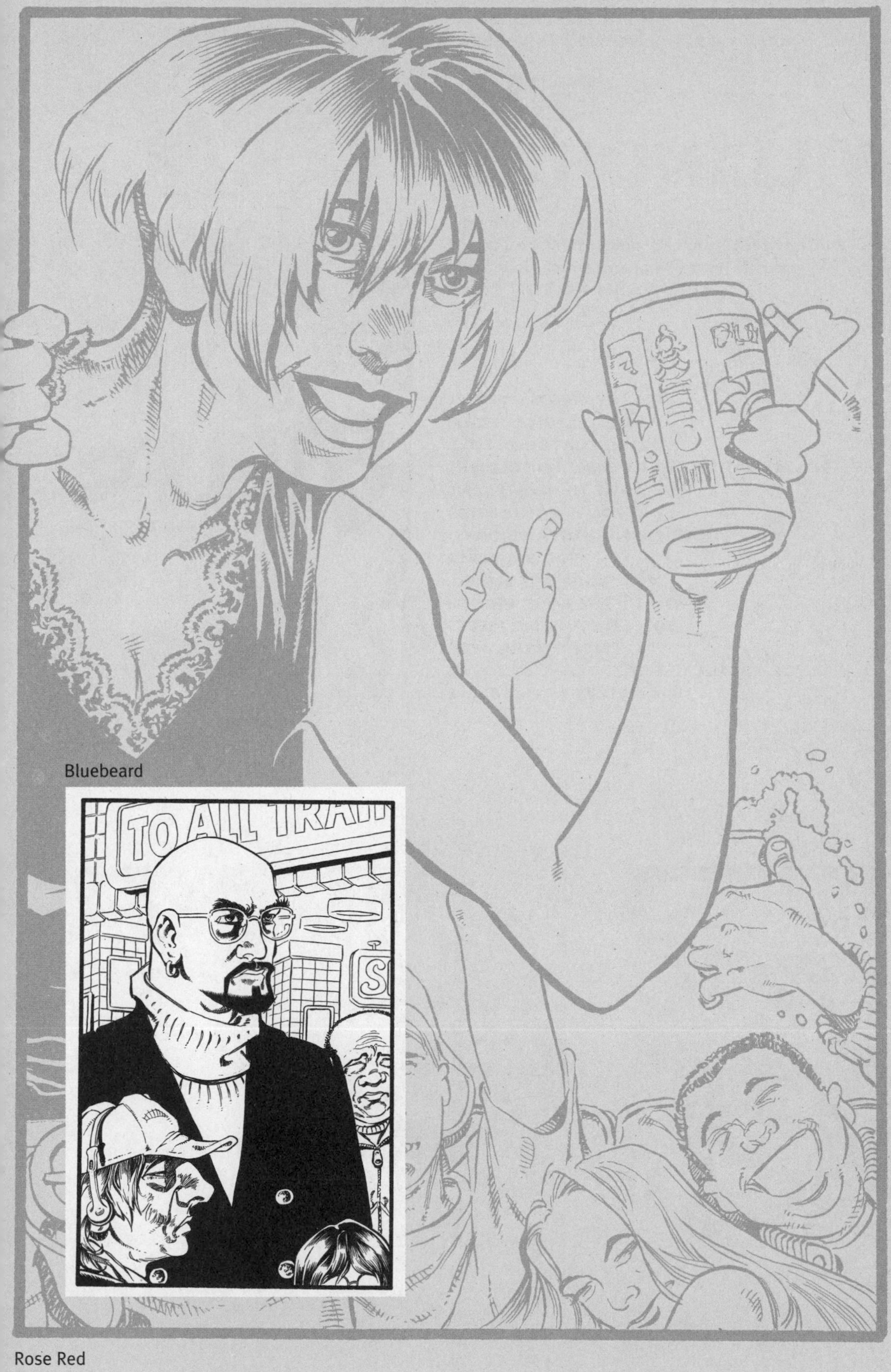
TO ALL

Bluebeard

Rose Red